156 059434

D0764742

D0736255

NOTHING TO

Also by Hugh Gregory Gallagher

FDR's Splendid Deception
Black Bird Fly Away: Disabled in an Able-Bodied World
By Trust Betrayed: Patients, Physicians and the License to Kill in the Third Reich
Etok: A Story of Eskimo Power
Advise and Obstruct: The Role of the United States Senate in Foreign Policy

NOTHING TO FEAR

FDR
IN PHOTOGRAPHS

HUGH GREGORY GALLAGHER

VANDAMERE PRESS

Published by
Vandamere Press
P.O. Box 17446
Clearwater, FL 33762
USA

Copyright 2001
Vandamere Press
ISBN 0-918339-56-1

All rights reserved, which includes the right to reproduce this book or any portion thereof in any form whatsoever, except as provided by U.S. Copyright Law. For information contact Vandamere Press. Printed in Canada.

*This book is
dedicated to
John Holstein*

Acknowledgments

There are many people who made this book possible: I would like to thank them all. Graphic designer Victor Weaver did a creative and painstaking job with the photos and the layout. John Ferris of the FDR Presidential Library was infinitely patient and conscientious in locating and copying the photos. The editorial assistance of Carol Talpers made the text both sharper and smoother. Pat Berger's copy editing saved me from many an egregious error. Patrick Folliard worked with me every step of the way. And my particular thanks must go to my publisher Art Brown and his associate John Cabin for their unrelenting patience and support.

I would like also to acknowledge and thank these institutions for their particular assistance: the Bethesda Naval Hospital; the Carl Vinson Institute, University of Georgia; the Lyndon Baines Johnson Presidential Library; the Little White House, Warm Springs, Georgia; and, as always, the Franklin D. Roosevelt Presidential Library for their extraordinary help and efficiency.

Table of Contents

Table of Contents (continued)

NOTHING TO FEAR

Franklin D. Roosevelt Presidential Library

Chapter *1*

President-elect Roosevelt

In the Great Depression of the 1930's, a third of America's workers had lost their jobs. Many were without food or shelter. In a famous photograph by Dorothea Lange, an unknown migrant woman lives in a tent with her seven children. She earns pennies, when she can, picking beans.

Inauguration day, March 4, 1933, dawned cold, gray and wet. Early in the morning, Eleanor Roosevelt, wife of the president elect, emerged from the Mayflower Hotel to walk her two dogs, Meggie and Major. The streets were empty and the trees were bare. American democracy faced its greatest crisis, hurtling toward catastrophe. Mrs. Roosevelt believed, "We are in a tremendous stream and none of us knows where we're going to land." She found the situation confronting her husband, "very, very grave and a little terrifying."

On that most dreary morning, Americans were exhausted, bitter and desperate. America had hit bottom. The economy was broken and no one knew how to fix it. Revolution was in the air. Whether revolution would come from the left or the right, no one knew. The nation was at the bottom of the worst depression it had ever experienced. The stock market had crashed, losing 89 percent of its value. One-third of the nation was out of work. Factory production had dropped by more than half. Eighty-eight percent of the nation's steel mills were idle. U.S. Steel, one of the largest companies in the country, simply shut its doors and fired its 225,000 workers. Small business was bankrupt.

Farmers were ruined. Crop prices, low throughout the decade, had now dropped to almost nothing. Harvest did not bring in enough revenue to pay for seed corn, let alone mortgage payments. Crops rotted in the fields; they were not worth picking. Banks foreclosed on the farmers and sold their land and equipment at auction, for pennies on the dollar. As if all these disasters were not enough, the Great Plains states were in drought, the worst drought in history. There was no rain, the wind blew, and terrifying dust storms, dark as night, swept across the prairies.

In towns, home owners could not make payments on their mortgages. Banks across the country foreclosed on loans, and then the banks failed. Back then, savings accounts were not insured. If your bank failed, you lost your money. Millions of Americans stormed the banks trying to withdraw their savings. There was simply not enough currency in circulation to cover the demand. In a single day, every bank in Chicago went bust. In Michigan, the governor ordered all banks to shut their doors. With their savings gone, millions of people, jobless and homeless for the first time, lived on the streets and depended on soup kitchens to stay alive. The city of Chicago was broke and paid its schoolteachers in scrip. People bartered for food and fuel; people paid for things with IOUs.

America, the hope of the world, was on its knees. American democracy, the great experiment, seemed doomed to failure. In 1933, there was no safety net to soften the blows of depression. There was no Social Security, no unemployment compensation, no minimum wage, no Medicare, no Medicaid, no housing subsidies, no food stamps. People were on their own. Former executives sold apples on street corners

to feed their children. Whole families, out of work and homeless, lived in shacks made of cardboard and tin cans. They called them Hoovervilles, after the president who was leaving office. Hundreds of thousands of hoboes roamed the country looking for work, begging for food, living under viaducts. Out-of-work miners in West Virginia smashed the windows of company stores to "steal" food to feed their children. Farmers in Iowa, on strike, refused to send their crops to market. Lynch mobs went after bankers. Food riots and bank stampedes were reported. Americans were starving.

Americans were desperate. Outgoing President Herbert Hoover, watched helplessly as the nation crumbled about him. Hoover was a good man, but he lacked the spirit and confidence necessary for leadership. He did his best. He began public works projects that provided jobs for some, but many, many more jobs were needed. He tried to save jobs by raising tariffs; but other countries raised theirs. United States exports fell and even more jobs were lost. When out-of-work veterans marched on Washington seeking help, the White House called on the army to disperse them. Americans watched in horror as General Douglas MacArthur, led the U. S. cavalry with sabers drawn. Tanks and steel-helmeted infantry with rifles and bayonets marched on the veterans and their families. Using force and tear gas, troops routed the vets and torched their camps. Millions were without food, yet President Hoover opposed using federal funds to feed the hungry.

The Depression was not limited to the United States. In other countries it spawned violence and revolt. In Russia, famine and slaughter resulted as dictator Stalin forced collectivization on Ukraine farmers. In Germany, Hitler and the

Nazi party seized control of the government. Even in Britain, a general strike had to be put down with force and bloodshed. Would America be next?

Franklin Delano Roosevelt was elected president November 8, 1932. As he went to bed the night of his victory, he murmured to his son, "I'm afraid I do not have the strength to do the job. Pray for me, Jimmy." Was he up to it? Political commentators had their doubts. During the campaign, columnist Walter Lippmann said Roosevelt was, "a pleasant man who, without any important qualifications for the office, would very much like to be president." He was "the weakest candidate since Franklin Pierce" added Washington pundit Charles Willis Thompson. They misjudged their man.

✳ ✳ ✳

At the stroke of noon, on March 4, 1933, the Marine Band, called "the President's Own," struck up "Hail to the Chief." The American government huddled on the inaugural platform in the cold March wind. President Hoover was there, along with his outgoing cabinet, the new cabinet, the Supreme Court, the Congress. More than 100,000 citizens looked on. The President-elect, a tall man leaning on the arm of his eldest son, James, appeared at the head of a ramp built for his use. Slowly he advanced to the lectern where the chief justice of the United States awaited. Franklin Delano Roosevelt, with his hand on the Bible, that had been in his family since the 1600s, was sworn in as the thirty-second president of the United States of America. Grasping the lectern, FDR turned to the microphones and to the American people. With a firm, calm voice and an almost magical projection of absolute confidence in America and himself, he began, "This is a day of national consecration . . ."

His voice rang out across Capitol Plaza and across America. "So first of all, let me assert my firm belief that the only thing we have to fear is fear itself — nameless, unreasoning, unjustified terror which paralyzes needed efforts to convert retreat into advance." Roosevelt promised to give "the great army of the people . . . a leadership of frankness and vigor." He said with a strength and determination no one could doubt, "I am the present instrument of their wishes." With the power the people had conferred on him, he said, he "would wage a war against the emergency as fiercely as against war itself."

FDR's inaugural address electrified the nation. The new secretary of labor, Frances Perkins, said it was like a great revival meeting. People in the crowd wept. Presidential advisor Raymond Moley, said, "Well, he's taken the ship of state and turned it right around." It changed everything..

Roosevelt had spoken of conquering fear and the paralysis it brings. Few noted that these were things he knew well. For in fact, FDR was paralyzed from the waist down and used a wheelchair. He could stand only with the help of long leg braces, leaning on the strong arm of a strong man, steadying himself with a cane.

A crippled America had chosen a crippled president to lead it.

Washington Post Co., Martin Luther King Public Library, Washington, D.C.

Washington Post Co., Martin Luther King Public Library, Washington, D.C.

In the Great Depression, American minorities suffered terribly. In the alleys of Washington, D.C., only blocks away from the White House, African Americans lived this way in 1933.

Franklin D. Roosevelt Presidential Library

In the 1930's, severe drought and rock-bottom crop prices drove families off their farms. Many left everything they had and set off for California in search of jobs. Here a migrant family, too poor for car or busfare, travels by foot along the highway.

Franklin D. Roosevelt Presidential Library

Franklin D. Roosevelt Presidential Library

March 4, 1933, President Franklin D. Roosevelt electrified the country with his inaugural address, and its most famous, "The only thing we have to fear is fear itself!" Roosevelt pledged an all out effort to feed the hungry and put people back to work. This great speech brought hope and confidence that, as FDR's campaign song had it, "Happy Days Are Here Again!" This is a popular poster of the time.

Within weeks, the federal government found temporary work for millions of workers. This is a Civilian Conservation Corps Camp where young unemployed homeless men were fed and housed as they worked in national parks and forests. In this photo, FDR has lunch with the CCC boys.

Franklin D. Roosevelt Presidential Library

Overnight, Eleanor and Franklin Roosevelt, here leading the inaugural parade, became the most popular people in America. Coverage of the dynamic Roosevelts and their activities dominated the press and the airwaves.

Franklin D. Roosevelt Presidential Library

Most Americans were not aware President Roosevelt was severely disabled. He could not stand or walk without assistance. To move about, he had to use a wheelchair. By an unwritten agreement, the media never mentioned the extent of his disability, nor did they ever publish a photo depicting his condition. This is one of only two known photos of FDR in his wheelchair.

Franklin D. Roosevelt Presidential Library

Chapter 2

Master Franklin Roosevelt

In this carefully posed 1898 photograph, nine year old Franklin is seated on his pony, Debby. With him is his father, James Roosevelt, on his mount, and his mother Sara, holding Franklin's dog, Monk. They are on the great East lawn of Springwood with its magnificent view over the Hudson River Valley. The house itself, a large frame Victorian mansion, was completely remodeled and expanded to FDR's wishes in 1927.

Franklin Delano Roosevelt was born January 30, 1882, at Springwood, the family estate in Hyde Park, New York. Both the Roosevelts and the Delanos, his mother Sara's family, had been prominent in New York social, business, and political life for more than two centuries. Both families were wealthy and privileged. Young Roosevelt was raised in a world now gone; with nannies and governesses, butlers and grooms, ponies and sailboats, and summers on the shore. His father, James Roosevelt, kept a private railroad car for the family's travel across the country. By the age of 14, the young Franklin had been to Europe eight times.

Franklin had a blessed childhood, surrounded by love and security. His father, a man in his fifties, led the life of a country squire. He spent much time with his son, teaching him to sail and ride. Together, the squire on his mount and young master Franklin on his pony would ride the Roosevelt estates. The father ingrained in Franklin the values, duties, and manners of a Victorian gentleman. FDR's mother, Sara, was a strong and vital woman. In her eyes, her beloved son could do no wrong. She wrapped him in love and, throughout her long life, was his advocate and support.

FDR grew up pampered and protected. He was educated at home and taken to play with children on other estates only under carefully monitored conditions. Nevertheless, his parents encouraged initiative and adventure, and nothing squelched his enthusiasm and good cheer. He did everything with gusto: sledding, skating, riding, hunting, fishing, sailing, stamp collecting, and collecting bird specimens.

Franklin's spirit can be found in the letters his mother so lovingly collected: "My dear Mama, We coasted [on sleds] yesterday, nothing dangerous yet, look out for tomorrow!! Your boy." His spirit can also be seen in the theme on ancient Egypt he wrote for his tutor, "The working people had nothing . . . The kings made them work so hard and gave them so little that by jingo! they nearly starved and by jinks! They had hardly any clothes so they died in quadrillions."

At the age of 12, he was given a rifle and taught to shoot. He began to collect one of each of the birds native to the Hudson River Valley. He would shoot them, skin them, and with assistance, stuff them. He labeled and mounted each one in a display case in the front hall of the Hyde Park mansion. They are there to this day. Young Franklin presented the New York Museum of Natural History with a pine grosbeak, a bird missing from their collection. In exchange, he was made the youngest member of the American Ornithologists Union.

One day, according to his mother, he came into the house to fetch his gun. He explained that he had seen a winter wren and was going to shoot it for his collection. "Do you think," she asked, "that wren is going to oblige you by sitting there while you come in to fetch your gun?" "Oh yes," Franklin replied, "he'll wait." And he did. That wren is now in the display case at Hyde Park.

The young Roosevelt had confidence; he also had the personal reserve expected of a young gentleman of his time. One summer at Campobello he was struck on the mouth with a stick. He lost one tooth, another was broken in half and a raw nerve was exposed to the air. Roosevelt did not complain of the pain. Indeed, he displayed neither discomfort nor emotion during the two hours it took to cross to the mainland to find a dentist. This was, his mother believed, entirely appropriate behavior and she was pleased her son went through the entire incident without fuss.

He was reserved, but he was not shy. When he played with other children, they liked him and he was a hearty participant in their games. Even in childhood, his mother noticed, he always seemed to end up the leader of the group. He was the one who gave the orders, which were, she said, "for reasons I have never been able to fathom," usually obeyed. When she pointed this out to him, he replied, "But Mommie, if I didn't give the orders, nothing would happen." Young Roosevelt was cheerful, confident and reserved. He was already a leader.

When FDR was five, the Roosevelts visited Washington, D.C. They took Franklin along when they paid a call on President Grover Cleveland, an old friend of James Roosevelt. The president looked down at the little boy and said, "My little man, I am making a strange wish for you. It is that you may never be the president of the United States."

Cleveland was not to get his wish.

✳ ✳ ✳

At the age of fourteen, FDR was sent to Groton, an Episcopal prep school for sons of the landed gentry. Its founder and rector, Endicott Peabody, was to play a major part in the formation of FDR's character. Peabody, educated in England, was a strict follower of the athletic Christianity of the day. Reverend Peabody believed in coal fires, cold showers, strenuous activity, a classical education, and a strict morality. Peabody sought for his boys the sound mind and sound body necessary for a life of religious faith and public service.

FDR was not pampered at Groton. Never having been exposed to large groups before, FDR promptly succumbed to the childhood diseases of his time. One after the other, he had the mumps, measles and scarlet fever. Roosevelt did not do particularly well in team sports. Boys of his social class were not expected to excel at their studies and he was no great student. Nevertheless, in his four years at Groton, FDR not only passed his high school courses, he also completed the first year of his college courses and won the Latin prize.

Roosevelt wanted to be a sea captain in the China trade, as his forebears had been. His parents thought otherwise and, at their insistence, he entered Harvard in the fall of 1900. He took it easy with his studies, never making much more than the gentlemanly Cs that were expected of him. He participated in campus activities. He was a cheerleader, and a class manager, and in his last year he was elected to the prestigious post of editor of the *Harvard Crimson*.

During Franklin's first semester at Harvard, his father died. Sara Roosevelt took over the management of the family investments and estates. She continued to run the family

affairs for the next 44 years. The marriage had been a close one and Sara felt deeply the loss of her husband. To soften her loss, she took an apartment in Boston to be near her cherished son. Although FDR was attentive to his mother and sometimes confided in her, Sara's presence did not seem to cramp his style. Roosevelt was a bon vivant, a man about town. He was charming and handsome. The girls adored him; and their mothers approved. Why not? FDR was well-bred, well-mannered, well-dressed—and he had money. He moved in the best circles of New York and Boston society. Weekends were a whirl of balls and house parties. He was a true "social butterfly" as they said in those days.

While at Harvard FDR began to develop an interest in politics. The Hyde Park Roosevelts had long been known as Democratic stalwarts. The other branch of the family, the Oyster Bay Roosevelts, were Republican. Their leader was Theodore Roosevelt. He had, in a few short years, been the dashing, reform-minded police commissioner of New York City, assistant secretary of the Navy, hero of the 1898 Spanish-American War, governor of New York state and vice president of the United States. In 1901, TR became the president of the United States. Throughout Franklin's childhood, he admired the vigor, the enthusiasm of his distant cousin, Teddy. Now Teddy was in the White House. Even though the Hyde Park Roosevelts were well-known Democrats, FDR campaigned for and, in 1904, cast his first presidential vote for his Republican cousin. Theodore Roosevelt, in many ways the first celebrity president, became immensely popular. Some of this popularity rubbed off on FDR. He became a regular at White House parties, and around Harvard, was known as "the cousin."

FDR took a liking to a tall, willowy girl with lustrous hair, beautiful eyes, and a perfect complexion. Her name was Eleanor Roosevelt. She was Franklin's distant cousin and President Theodore Roosevelt's favorite niece. Eleanor had been at school in England during her teen-age years and now was "out" in New York society. Eleanor's childhood had been a bitter one. Her mother, Anna Eleanor Hall, a famous and unhappy beauty, thought her daughter ugly and called her Granny and the ugly duckling. When Eleanor was eight, her mother died. Her little brother died of scarlet fever the following year, and then, when she was ten, her alcoholic father, Elliott Roosevelt, died. She loved her father dearly, even though he had often abandoned her. Now he had abandoned her forever. The orphaned Eleanor went to live, in the words of biographer Frank Freidel, "with a neurotic aunt and an alcoholic uncle in the household of a stern grandmother."

At fifteen, Eleanor was sent to Allenwood, an English boarding school, run by Mlle. Marie Souvestre, an early advocate of women's rights. Under that teacher's tutelage, Eleanor blossomed. Eleanor traveled all over Europe with her. She learned to speak French and spoke it fluently throughout her life. Eleanor was a good student, and she found to her surprise, that she was extremely popular with the other girls. Eleanor was different from the other debutantes. She had a serious side and a social conscience, unusual for a girl of her age and era. At the age of 19, she was helping tenement dwellers in the Hell's Kitchen part of New York, teaching at the Irvington Street Settlement House and investigating the conditions of women workers for the Consumer League. Even as they were dating, Eleanor took Franklin around to show him the hardship and suffering of the city's poor.

The couple fell deeply in love. FDR courted her assiduously, coming down from Harvard almost every other weekend. He escorted her to the Harvard-Yale football game, the big event of the college year. His doting mother knew nothing of their relationship. In November 1903, after they attended chapel at Groton where Eleanor's brother was a student, Franklin asked her to marry him and she accepted. She thought of an Elizabeth Barrett Browning poem, "Unless you can swear, 'For life, for death!'/ Oh, fear to call it loving!" His pledge to her, quoting from another poem, was to "be faithful unto death."

His mother was not happy. "Franklin gave me quite a startling announcement," she wrote in her diary. They were so young—Eleanor was nineteen, he was twenty-one. Sara Roosevelt tried to keep the couple apart, to keep them from meeting so often. Sara even took her son on a six-week Caribbean cruise in the middle of the academic term. It was all to no avail. Giving in to her beloved son, as she always did, she told him, "I must try to be unselfish and, of course, dear child, I do rejoice in your happiness and will not put any stones or straws in the way of it."

Theodore Roosevelt, was absolutely delighted. He loved Eleanor as though she was his own daughter. On March 4, 1905, TR was inaugurated to a second term. On March 17, he came up to New York, led the St. Patrick's Day parade down Fifth Avenue, and in the afternoon, acting as stand-in for his late brother, walked Eleanor down the aisle at her wedding. The ceremony was held at the President's Manhattan townhouse. Groton Rector Endicott Peabody performed the ceremony. Theodore Roosevelt, the twenty-seventh president of the United States, gave the hand of his niece, Eleanor Roosevelt, to Franklin Roosevelt, a man who was to become the thirty-second president of the United States. "There's nothing like keeping the name in the family," remarked TR.

✳ ✳ ✳

The newlyweds sailed for a three month honeymoon in Europe. On the return voyage, Eleanor discovered that she was pregnant. While they were gone, Eleanor's mother-in-law, Sara, rented a brownstone rowhouse for them in Manhattan and furnished it according to her own tastes. She also hired and paid for a staff of three to run the house. As a Christmas present to the couple, Sara announced that she was building two five-story adjoining townhouses on 65th Street—one for them and one for her. The houses would have connecting doors at every level.

Franklin thought this arrangement was splendid. He was in his second year at Columbia Law School. After passing the bar, he dropped out of law school and entered Carter, Ledyard and Milburn, a prominent corporate law firm on Wall Street. He maintained an active social life with his wife and mother, as well as late nights on the town and Saturday poker games with the boys.

Eleanor gave birth six times in the following twelve years. One child died in infancy, leaving the couple five children: daughter Anna and sons James, Franklin Jr., John, and Elliott. Franklin sailed on, quite above the difficulties Eleanor found in managing the babies and directing a coterie of nurses, governesses, and an enlarged household staff. Most irritating of all was her ever-present, interfering mother-in-law. When Franklin asked his wife what was wrong, she burst into tears. She sobbed that she "did not like to live in a house that was not mine, one that I had done nothing about and which did not represent the way I wanted to live." Franklin liked their living arrangements and he dismissed his wife's complaints as nonsense.

Much later in her life, Eleanor Roosevelt wrote (but did not publish) that her mother-in-law was "determined to bend the marriage to the way she wanted it to be. What she wanted was to hold onto Franklin and his children; she wanted them to grow as she wished. As it turned out [the children] were more my mother-in-law's than they were mine." As in her childhood, Eleanor felt unloved and kept all her resentment swallowed up inside herself.

The family spent weekends, often weeks at Hyde Park, where Sara was head of household. The servants referred to Sara as Mrs. Roosevelt and Eleanor as Mrs. Eleanor. This continued throughout their lives, even when Eleanor was the first lady of the land. At dinner, Franklin took his father's place at the head of the table, with Sara at its foot. Eleanor sat in between with the children. After dinner, Franklin would take one of the two armchairs beside the fireplace in the drawing room, his mother would take the other. Eleanor sat on a pillow or footstool between them.

FDR's law work was not taxing. He kept at it for three years, but it did not hold his interest. He dreamed of following in the footsteps of his "Uncle" Teddy. FDR mused to an officemate one day that he thought he had a shot at the presidency. First, he would get elected to the state legislature, and then he would wangle an appointment as assistant secretary of the Navy, as Teddy had done. He could then get elected governor. After that, he said, "anyone who is governor of New York has a good chance to be president, with any luck." Especially if his name is Roosevelt.

※ ※ ※

Franklin's family home was in the town of Hyde Park in Dutchess County on the east side of the Hudson river north of New York City. The counties on the east side contained the wealthy gentry with their mansions on the bluffs high above the river; most of them were Republican. Further inland were the farmers, mostly of old Dutch descent, who were also Republican. Only the town of Poughkeepsie was safely Democratic. The Roosevelts were wealthy, and they had a big house on the river. They were also an old Dutch family, but they were Democratic.

Young Roosevelt drew the attention of the Democratic party officials. He was Dutch and he was Democratic. He shared the name of the now former President Roosevelt, at the time the most popular man in the nation. FDR was good-looking, personable, and more important, he had the money to finance his own campaign. The story has it that one day in front of a Poughkeepsie bank, the local Democratic committee chairman asked FDR to be a candidate in the 1908 election. FDR replied that he would like to talk to his mother first before giving an answer. The chairman then said, "Frank, the men who are looking out of that window are waiting for an answer. They won't like to hear that you had to ask your mother." "I'll take it," FDR responded. He was 28 and now a candidate for the New York State senate.

Political experts said young Roosevelt had no better than a one-in-five chance of winning, but FDR was lucky. The Republican administration in Washington had angered the farmers. Furthermore, the New York Republican party was split in a bitter struggle between the progressive TR forces and the old guard conservatives. The old guard had been riddled with well-publicized scandals, and FDR's conservative opponent had been linked to the scandals.

The campaign was only a month long, but FDR took to it with all the vigor of his Uncle Ted. He rented a red Maxwell convertible, covered it with banners and pennants, and drove throughout the district, speaking wherever he found a few people gathered. The automobile was still a new-fangled thing that scared the horses. Whenever Roosevelt met up with a farmer's horse and wagon, he would have to stop the Maxwell and turn off its engine. This, of course, gave him an opportunity to strike up a conversation with the farmer.

Roosevelt's speeches drew attention. He spoke with a nasal upperclass accent. He wore little pince-nez glasses on his nose and tilted his head back when he spoke. This gave him the appearance of being a snob, of looking down his nose at people. The old politicians began to call him "The Young Duke."

Roosevelt campaigned against political machines and party bosses; he called for reform. His platform was vague, but his enthusiasm was convincing. To everyone's surprise, on election day he won handily, carrying his hometown 406 to 258. He was the first Democrat to win the seat since 1856. When party boss "Big Tim" Sullivan of the Bowery learned that a Roosevelt had been elected, he was upset. "You know these Roosevelts," he moaned, "This fellow is young. Wouldn't it be safer to drown him before he grows up?"

As the new state senator, FDR was determined to make a name for himself. Most legislators commuted to the state capitol, Albany, or stayed in a rented room during legislative sessions. Not Roosevelt: he rented a large house and moved his wife, children, nannies, and maids to Albany. He would be a full-time senator. Eleanor and Franklin used their house for meetings and entertaining New York officials and legislators. Soon they were acknowledged as active players in the political game.

Before 1913, U. S. senators were selected by the senate of each state. In the early days of his first session, FDR took on the leadership of a group of Democrats determined to defeat the man Tammany Hall (the powerful Democratic machine of New York City) had selected to be senator from New York. There was a terrific scrap that made headlines across the country. Ultimately, the rebel group had to compromise. But FDR had established himself as a "comer," someone willing to take on the old-time bosses.

Roosevelt learned some powerful lessons during his years in the state senate. He learned that in politics, you can't always get what you want. Lofty statements of principle may get you publicity, but they will not win many votes on the senate floor. Honorable men can disagree and the opinions of dishonorable men cannot be ignored. To be effective you have to persuade, flatter, and give as well as take. Better to get half a loaf now than to hold out for a whole loaf—and get nothing. As Uncle Ted told Franklin, "I would be glad to play with the angels but the angels are not playing around just now." FDR's record in the state senate was a progressive one;

he was an effective supporter of workers' rights, primaries for the nomination of party candidates, popular elections to choose U.S. Senators, and with the strong support of Eleanor, women's suffrage.

In 1912, Roosevelt ran for a second term in the state senate. On the opening day of the month-long campaign, FDR was flat on his back in bed with a serious case of typhoid fever. In an effort to keep his name before the public, he hired Albany newsman Louis Howe. Howe flooded the newspapers with press releases and statements, plastered posters around the district, and passed out brochures, all flattering to FDR.

It was a good year for Democrats. The Republican party nominated William Howard Taft for a second term as president. Former president Theodore Roosevelt bolted the Republican party, taking with him a large number of his progressive followers. He declared his candidacy for president on the Bull Moose ticket. TR split the Republican vote, and a progressive Democrat, Woodrow Wilson, won the White House.

FDR was reelected to the state senate, even though he had not made a single speech or public appearance. Many Republicans crossed over to vote for him because of the power of his name and the appeal of his progressive policies. During the campaign, Howe sent FDR a note addressed to the "Beloved and revered future president." Howe wasn't kidding. He meant it. Howe spent the rest of his life working to make Franklin Roosevelt president.

Franklin D. Roosevelt Presidential Library

Franklin at the age of four on the Hyde Park estate. He and his white dog are riding on the back of a slow paced mule. Franklin is dressed in his "silks and sashes"—bonnet, dress with lace, white stockings and patent leather shoes. This is the way young boys were dressed back in the 1880s.

Franklin D. Roosevelt Presidential Library

Young Franklin was taught to sail at an early age. Here he is, at the age of 6, at the wheel of his father's yacht, in the Bay of Fundy, New Brunswick, Canada.

In this studio pose, Franklin is with his mother, Sara Roosevelt, in Washington, D.C., 1887. Franklin met President Cleveland, in the Oval Office, on this visit. He is five and has graduated from frilly dresses to a more manly kilt.

On the same visit, Franklin posed with his father, James Roosevelt. Born to wealth, James was a gentleman squire who tended his estate and dabbled in railroads on Wall Street. Notice that he is wearing the Roosevelt family signet ring on his finger. After his death, the ring passed to FDR and then to his son James.

Franklin D. Roosevelt Presidential Library

Franklin D. Roosevelt Presidential Library

As a youth, FDR was rather spindly—his tall frame had not yet filled out. Although he never excelled in team sports, he was an active outdoorsman, as shown in these photographs.

Eight year old Franklin stands at the stern of his sailboat. He also had an iceboat for sailing on the Hudson. He skated, tobogganed, and used a horse drawn sleigh in the winter time.

Young Roosevelt competes in a trotting race at a Dutchess County fair. He was a skilled horseman who often accompanied his father as they rode the bounds of their Hyde Park estate.

Franklin, at the age of 17, stands with his golf clubs. He was an ardent golfer, only giving up the game at the onset of his polio. This picture is taken at Campobello, the site of the Roosevelt summer cottage.

Franklin D. Roosevelt Presidential Library

Franklin D. Roosevelt Presidential Library

Franklin D. Roosevelt Presidential Library

Franklin was an all right student at his prep school, Groton. Although not outstanding, he was popular enough. Here is is as manager of the second string football team.

Franklin D. Rossevelt Presidential Library

Full of beans and testosterone, FDR hams it up with the girls for the camera. He is 20, at a society party in Barrytown, New York, in 1902.

Franklin D. Rossevelt Presidential Library

Franklin D. Rossevelt Presidential Library

At Harvard, FDR was popular and sought after. He was called "The Cousin", as his cousin, Teddy Roosevelt, was president of the United States. Here, in his senior year, he is shown in his prestigious post as editor of the Harvard Crimson.

Franklin D. Rossevelt Presidential Library

This is Eleanor Roosevelt, nee Roosevelt, in her wedding dress. She had the popular "Gibson girl" look of the era—wasp waist, puffy sleeves, lustrous hair piled high. There are no photos of the wedding itself, which is probably just as well. Eleanor's uncle, President Theodore Roosevelt, walked her down the aisle and completely stole the show.

Franklin D. Rossevelt Presidential Library

The Roosevelts went to Europe on the "Grand Tour" for their honeymoon. Over three months, they visited Britain, France, Italy, Switzerland and Germany. Here they are, enjoying themselves and visiting friends at Strathpeffer, Scotland.

Franklin D. Rossevelt Presidential Library

In 1910, FDR made a run for a seat in the New York State Senate. Few expected him to win. He had an upperclass accent and an arrogant way of carrying himself, with his head back, peering down at people through his pince-nez eye glasses—as is seen in this photograph. The old politicians called him "The Young Duke." Roosevelt fooled them all: he criss-crossed the district in a zippy bright-red convertible, speaking at ever crossroad and shaking every hand he could reach. He became a State Senator at the age of 28.

On the honeymoon, Franklin took along one of the new Kodak Brownie cameras. Here is his photograph of Eleanor intently reading a newspaper aboard a gondola in Venice. Notice Eleanor is holding her husband's straw boater as he takes the photo.

Franklin D. Rossevelt Presidential Library

Franklin D. Roosevelt Presidential Library

Chapter *3*

F. D. Roosevelt,
Assistant Secretary of the Navy

When Woodrow Wilson became president in 1913, he asked FDR to serve as assistant secretary of the navy. This was an important post for a young man just turned 31. His Uncle Ted had served in the same position on his rise to the White House. FDR loved the job. He was especially fond of his official duties — visiting navy bases, inspecting ships, reviewing troops.

Franklin Roosevelt supported the candidacy of Woodrow Wilson for president of the United States, over the objections of the Tammany Hall bosses. In fact, FDR spearheaded Wilson's campaign throughout the state. Thus, it was no surprise when Wilson appointed 31 year old FDR as assistant secretary of the Navy. In doing so, Wilson brushed aside the warning of New York Senator Elihu Root: "You know the Roosevelts, don't you? Whenever a Roosevelt rides, he rides in front." When young Franklin was asked if he would like the job, he replied, "I would like it more than anything in the world." And no wonder: Uncle Ted had held the same job from 1895 through 1898 and by 1901 he was President of the United States.

The young Roosevelts fitted easily into the Washington scene of 1912. Both Eleanor and Franklin had visited the capital many times when Uncle Ted was in the White House. They were already friends with the town's leading figures: Senator Henry Cabot Lodge; Justice Oliver Wendell Holmes; Justice Brandeis; the gloomy literary sage Henry Adams; and Ambassadors Jusserand of France and Cecil-Rice of Britain. The Roosevelts quickly made friends with the new Wilson appointees. The couple was popular in both Democratic and Republican circles. Social protocol was strict in those days; there were many rules that could not be broken. Eleanor found that she was required to make twenty "calls" a day. At each home, she had to chat a minute or two. If no one was "at home," she left her card, bent at the corner to indicate she had called in person. Soon invitations and thank-you notes and such became so burdensome that she was forced to employ a social secretary three mornings a week to help with the correspondence. Eleanor hired a charming, vivacious girl of good family named Lucy Mercer.

Roosevelt wrote his mother on his first day at his new job, "I am baptized, confirmed, sworn in, vaccinated—and somewhat at sea!" He was not at sea for long. FDR dived into his job and loved it. He was number 2 at the Navy Department. Soon enough he had, as he said, "his fingers in every pie."

FDR's boss, Secretary of the Navy Josephus Daniels, was a small-town Southern gentleman, deeply religious, a populist, a pacifist, and a racist. Daniels wore a string tie, black suits in the winter, white in the summer. Young Franklin had never met anyone like Daniels and called him the "funniest looking hillbilly" he ever saw. Daniels strongly disapproved of drink and fornication. He forbade wine to be served in officer messes and refused distribution of condoms to sailors for fear it would encourage them toward "an evil which perverts their morals." He also wanted sailors to wear pajamas. Such beliefs did not make him popular.

Daniels and Franklin, opposites in so many ways, worked together as a team for seven years. FDR's family had made their fortunes sailing clipper ships in the China trade. They had been seafarers for generations. Franklin had grown up reading books on naval history and was an accomplished yachtsman.

Secretary Daniels knew nothing about the navy; FDR knew a lot. Daniels, however, knew more than he let on. He was shrewd, intelligent, and politically savvy. He was slow and careful. Most important, he was a favorite of the Congress. Franklin learned a lot from Daniels about how Washington works. Roosevelt came to respect his boss and the two became lifelong friends.

Daniels took a paternal interest in young Franklin. It was "love at first sight," he once wrote. Daniels was proud to have appointed FDR as assistant secretary. "His distinguished cousin TR went from that place to the presidency. May history repeat itself," Daniels wrote in his diary. Franklin was impetuous and impatient, sometimes even reckless. His actions often skirted insubordination, but Secretary Daniels retained the support of President Wilson and firm control of his department and many a time kept FDR out of trouble.

Roosevelt brought Louis Howe down to Washington to work as his assistant. Howe was good at administrative details and had a keen political eye. His most important role, however, was to act as FDR's press agent. Throughout Roosevelt's tenure at Navy, Howe ground out press releases. With Howe's help, Franklin D. Roosevelt's name and face were often seen in the papers.

In 1913, the U.S. Navy had 65,000 men and a budget of $150 million. The two great naval powers were Britain and Germany. The U.S. fleet, no match, was even smaller than Argentina's. From the first, FDR was a "big navy" man, working to enlarge the fleet. This goal set him apart from his conservative boss and made him the favorite of the navy's officer corps.

In 1914, war broke out in Europe. England, France and

Russia were on one side and Germany and the Austro-Hungarian Empire were on the other. Roosevelt, like many others, believed that America would be dragged into the war at some point. He knew the U.S. Navy was woefully unprepared for such an event. For three years, Wilson steered America along a path of strict neutrality. In spite of increasing provocation, Wilson refused to be provoked. He said, "There is such a thing as . . . being too proud to fight." This policy was hard to swallow for those who saw America's involvement in the war as inevitable. As FDR wrote his wife, "I just know I shall do some awful unneutral thing before I get through."

Wilson insisted that the Navy stay at status quo levels so as not to antagonize Britain or Germany. As a result, when America finally entered the war on Britain's side in April 1917, the United States fleet had only 267 ships in commission, but America armed itself with astonishing speed. By the end of the war, November 11, 1918, the Navy had 2,000 ships in commission and 500,000 men on duty. FDR was not solely responsible for this rapid buildup but he played an important role. He had become, said the *New York Times,* "the man to see" in the Navy Department.

Roosevelt learned how to get things done. For example, the Argentine Navy had commissioned the construction of four ships at the Massachusetts shipyard owned by Charles B. Schwab, Bethlehem Steel's CEO. Schwab would not release the ships until the Argentines had paid for them in full. Argentina was an ally and needed the ships right away. FDR met with Schwab's young assistant, Joseph P. Kennedy. "Don't worry about the money," FDR assured Kennedy, "The State Department will make them pay." Kennedy replied that Mr. Schwab had said that no ship would be delivered until the Argentines paid for it. "Why that's absurd," said Roosevelt. "No dice," answered Kennedy. Walking Kennedy to the door, arm around his shoulder, FDR said it was nice to have met him and that Kennedy should drop by anytime he was in Washington. And, Roosevelt added, "If the ships are not released at once, I will send tugboats to get them." Kennedy went back to his boss and advised him to call FDR's bluff. "He's just a four flusher," said Kennedy. Several days later, the tugboats arrived. The ships were towed out into the harbor, boarded by Argentine crews, and sailed away.

Kennedy was born of poor Irish immigrants. Roosevelt's family had been landed gentry since before the Revolutionary War. The two men did not like each other. Starting with the tugboats, an antagonism developed between the two families that was to last more than 50 years, even through the presidency of Joseph's son, John F. Kennedy.

Roosevelt went to Europe in July of 1918. He was the highest ranking official to visit Britain and France since the United States had entered the war in April of 1917. He was royally wined and dined. In London, he met with the British prime minister Lloyd George; the foreign secretary, Lord Balfour; and the first lord of the admiralty. FDR also had an hour and a half meeting with King George V, whose wife, Queen Mary, was a friend of FDR's mother. In Paris, he met with Premier Clemenceau.

FDR was in Europe to inspect U.S. Navy installations, which he did most thoroughly In addition, he went to the front lines in France. He was under artillery fire. He saw the rotting bodies of soldiers and horses, their blood pooling in the mud amidst the wreckage of battle. He tramped the field of Verdun, where the French had lost 300,000 men in a single battle. He was deeply impressed by what he saw.

With the entry of the United States on the Allied side, the war in Europe became World War I. The war, which lasted four years, was long and bloody. It was waged from trenches along a fixed line 1,200 miles long.. Each side was firmly dug in, well fixed to massacre the other with machine gun and poison gas, should it attempt to gain advantage by "going over the top." An entire generation of European men were sacrificed in futile offensives and still, all was stalemate.

The arrival of the American Expeditionary Force ended this stalemate. More than a million American men went into battle. American resources provided an endless supply of arms and munitions. Even more important was the leadership of Woodrow Wilson. Until the entry of America, the war had been fought for no purpose. It was just a war brought on by alliances and mistakes. Wilson, with inspired words, defined the Allied cause: "The world must be made safe for democracy." This was, he said, "A war to end all wars."

Wilson called for "a peace without victory." "Only a peace between equals can last," he said. To bring this about, "A general association of nations must be formed . . . of great and small nations alike." He called for "such a concert of free peoples as shall bring peace and safety to all nations and make the world itself at last free." This was a cause to fight for. Wilson's words gave reason for sacrifice.

His words electrified the nations, gave courage to the Allies, and brought hope even to the peoples of the enemy. Millions of copies of Wilson's speeches were dropped behind enemy lines. Cynics called Wilson an idealist, but he replied," Well, that is the way I know I am an American. America is the only idealistic nation in the world."

The Allied forces overwhelmed the enemy, and the Great War ended not in surrender but in armistice. Britain's wily Lloyd George, France's stubborn Clemenceau, and Wilson met in a great peace conference at Versailles in 1919, to work out the terms of the peace treaty and the Covenant of the League of Nations. When Wilson arrived in Europe, he was received as no man in history, before or after, has been received. Millions upon millions cheered him as he rode through the streets of London, Paris, and Rome.

Roosevelt returned to Europe and spent time with the American delegation at the peace conference. He was witness as America was sabotaged by the secret treaties, by the avarice and bitterness of the European politicians. He saw the naive United States forced into compromise after compromise as Wilson fought to save the League of Nations. But at home, he made the mistake of turning the League into a partisan issue. Roosevelt watched as Wilson was bullied in Europe and faced rebuke in America. FDR accompanied Wilson on board the USS *Washington,* as he returned to America to present his badly flawed treaties to the U.S. Senate for ratification. Roosevelt always remembered Wilson telling him on the voyage, "The United States must go in [the League] or it will break the heart of the world, for she is the only nation that all feel is disinterested and all trust."

Wilson fought hard for the treaties, but they were rejected by the Senate. The world's heart was broken and Wilson's too. He suffered a series of strokes and died shortly thereafter. As president, Franklin Roosevelt had a portrait of Wilson hung on the wall of the Cabinet Room—to remind him of Wilson's great vision and to remind him that vision is nothing without the political skill and the support needed to back it up.

Franklin D. Roosevelt Presidential Library

During the years before World War I, in the hot summer months, the young assistant secretary was able to get away from Washington for weeks at a time to join the family at their summer cottage on Campobello Island. Here is the family on a picnic outing via canoe, with two Indians paddling. FDR paddles his own canoe.

Franklin D. Roosevelt Presidential Library

The water was cold at Campobello and the beach was rocky but that did not stop the Roosevelts. Here Eleanor in serge wool swimming cap and proper beach robe waits while Franklin shakes the gravel out his rubber swim shoes.

Franklin D. Rossevelt Presidential Library

The Roosevelt family was growing. Here they are shown at Campobello. Notice that Eleanor is looking down rather than at the camera. This is true of many of the early photos. She hated to be photographed because not only was she still shy but she also considered herself to be ugly.

Franklin D. Roosevelt Presidential Library

With American entry into World War I, FDR became the "man to see" in the Navy Department. Here the dapper assistant secretary confers with two officers wearing the old "choker" naval winter uniform.

Franklin D. Roosevelt Presidential Library

This is the assistant secretary at a war bond rally in 1918. He is standing beside famous early movie actors Douglas Fairbanks and Mary Pickford, with Charlie Chaplin and Marie Dressler kneeling in the foreground.

During the War, Washington executives performed calisthenics every morning before work so as to be in good physical shape should they be called to active military service. That's FDR at the far right.

Franklin D. Rossevelt Presidential Library

Government executives also regularly practiced target shooting in case they should be called to fight in the front-line trenches. Here is FDR at the rifle range, Waldorf, Maryland.

Franklin D. Rossevelt Presidential Library

Franklin D. Roosevelt Presidential Library

Throughout the Washington years, FDR's longtime assistant, Louis Howe, acted as a press agent, arranging publicity for the ambitious young Roosevelt. This is from a magazine story about how much he enjoyed pipe smoking—FDR smoked cigarettes.

Franklin D. Roosevelt Presidential Library

Chapter *4*

Husband and Candidate

Assistant Secretary of the Navy Roosevelt was the first Cabinet-level officer to visit Europe after America joined World War I in 1917. Here he is seen, properly togged up, riding in an open car in London. During his visit, he called on King George V, Prime Minister Lloyd-George of Britain and Premier Clemenceau of France.

During his voyage home from Europe in 1918, FDR contracted a serious case of the influenza. When he got home, it was diagnosed as double pneumonia. In the days before antibiotics, this was a serious matter. Perhaps even more serious was Eleanor's discovery, while unpacking his suitcase, of love letters between Franklin and her social secretary, Lucy Mercer. Franklin recovered, but Eleanor never did.

Eleanor was deeply hurt by the discovery. The man who had sworn to love her "For life! For death!", had betrayed her. She had borne him six children, the last one only two years before. She had worked day and night to advance his career. She was devoting nine, ten hours a day to organizing navy wives in volunteer war work. She thought she and Franklin were a team, and now he had betrayed her.

Their marriage was difficult. Certainly, they loved each other. They shared a deep commitment to work to make the world a better place. They both were reserved in their behavior and repressed emotionally. Neither had much knowledge of sex. Eleanor was ill at ease with fun and she disapproved of alcohol. She called herself a Puritan. She had what she called her Griselda times, times when she would sink into gloom and depression. Franklin certainly had his serious side but he liked to play too. He was handsome and debonair. He was gregarious and happy; he loved his booze and his parties. He loved to flirt. Women adored him and men admired him.

The Roosevelts tended to absorb people. Louis Howe gave up his career and lived away from his family to be with Franklin and further his career. In the five years she had been with them, Lucy Mercer, too, had become a part of the Roosevelts' lives. In later years there would be many others who believed in the Roosevelts and what they were working to achieve. These people dedicated their lives to the couple.

Lucy was a social equal, descended from the Carolls of Maryland, and the Roosevelts were comfortable with her. She filled in for them if an extra woman was needed at a dinner party. She babysat the children and went with the family on picnics and cruises on the Potomac. She helped oversee the running of the Roosevelts' household staff of eight and, during the war, helped to organize and run Eleanor's volunteer work. In those years, there was no air-conditioning. Summers in Washington are very hot and humid. During the summer months, Eleanor would take the children up to the family "cottage" at Campobello Island just off the coast of Maine. Franklin, busy at the navy, would come up as he could, for several days, once or twice a summer. Lucy remained in Washington.

The romance began innocently enough. Franklin wrote often to his family, recounting what he was doing: "Such a funny party, but it worked out wonderfully! The Charlie Magnus, the Cary Graysons, Lucy Mercer and Nigel Law, and they all got on splendidly." He also wrote, "off in car at 2:30 to the Horsey's place near Harper's Ferry. Lucy Mercer went and the Graysons and we got there at 5:30."

As time went on, Lucy and Franklin were sometimes seen alone together in the car. In those days it was considered shocking for a married man to be alone with a woman not his wife. Roosevelt's relatives, living in Washington, buzzed among themselves about what was happening but said nothing to Eleanor. Cousin Alice Roosevelt Longworth, the cruelest tongue in town, a woman who would say anything to hurt Eleanor, believed that Lucy and Franklin were in love, but she never believed they had consummated their love. Other family members believed they had. No one knows.

But the love letters were real. Eleanor confronted her husband. The crisis peaked at a painful family meeting: Eleanor offered Franklin a divorce. His mother Sara said that if they divorced, she would cut her son off from all the family money. Louis Howe said that divorce would ruin Franklin's political career. Franklin cared deeply about his wife and children; he did not want a divorce. Eleanor agreed to remain his wife, raise his children, and continue to play her role as Mrs. Roosevelt in society and political life—but she would no longer share their marriage bed. Franklin must agree never to see Miss Mercer again. And so, it was agreed.

The marriage held. They picked up the pieces of their relationship and went on. Certain it is, that from this experience, FDR learned how much he loved his wife and children.

Many years later, Eleanor told friends that the Mercer affair had taught her that she could not allow herself to be completely dependent on the love of Franklin. She must build a role and a life of her own For her own self-esteem, she must stand on her own two feet. Years after her husband's death, Eleanor wrote, "All human beings have failings, all human beings have needs, temptations, and stresses. Men and women who live together for many long years get to know one another's failings; but they also come to know what is worthy of respect and admiration in those they live with and in themselves." Close friends believed she never stopped loving Franklin.

In the aftermath of the affair, Franklin tried extra hard to be considerate of Eleanor's feelings and she responded in kind. Leaving the children in the care of Sara, the couple sailed for Europe in 1919 and, by all reports, had a marvelous time together.

In February 1920, Lucy Mercer married Winthrop Rutherfurd. The two had six children and lived happily together until his death in 1942.

✳ ✳ ✳

There were no strong candidates for the presidential nominations in 1920. The Republicans, after much stirring around, nominated an affable nonentity named Warren G. Harding. As a Republican senator reported, "There weren't any first raters this year, so we picked the best of the second raters." President Wilson was serving out his term, a sad, invalid recluse in the White House. He had been a powerful leader in World War I; but now the people seemed tired of him and his idealism. Harding, as ordinary a man as you could find, perfectly reflected the mood of the voters when he called for a "return to normalcy."

The Democrats settled on James Cox, who was like Harding, a newspaper editor from Ohio. Cox was as colorless as Harding and not as good-looking. To enliven the ticket, party officials picked Franklin D. Roosevelt as vice presidential nominee. Thanks to Howe's press releases, FDR had become nationally known. He had a famous name, he was as personable and energetic as TR, and he was photogenic. At the Democratic convention in San Francisco, FDR had made headlines by forcibly wrestling the New York standard away from Tammany delegates, so as to march with it during the floor demonstration for Wilson.

During the campaign, FDR crisscrossed the country by private railroad car. He made over 1,000 speeches, sometimes as many as seven a day. He met city and state officials, party bigwigs, newspaper publishers, and businessmen. Howe kept a card index of the people FDR met, compiling a mailing list that was to be invaluable in the future. Roosevelt loved every minute of the campaign. He liked the attention, the applause, and the "bully pulpit" it gave him to speak out on the issues. His young duke manner of speaking became less affected, more informal and genuine. At the election, the Cox-Roosevelt ticket was defeated by a landslide. Nevertheless, in the ten short years since he had entered politics, FDR had established himself as a rising young Democrat on the national scene. He had become someone to watch. Many thought he would cop the Democratic nomination in 1924. "The day when will come," predicted a Harvard classmate, "when you will come to be our father in the White House." Back in 1907, Roosevelt had said he thought he had a good chance to be president, "with any luck." So far, FDR's luck was holding.

Franklin D. Rossevelt Presidential Library

While in Europe he visited the frontline where he came under enemy artillery fire. He also inspected U. S. Navy facilities. Here he is piped on board the battleship USS New York.

Franklin D. Rossevelt Presidential Library

Inspecting a U. S. Naval installation at Gironda, France.

Franklin D. Rossevelt Presidential Library

At the U. S. Naval Air Station, Pauillac, France.

Franklin D. Roosevelt Presidential Library

Returning from Europe, FDR is greeted by his children, Anna and Franklin, Jr. He returned with a bad case of flu, which developed into pneumonia, a life-threatening illness in the days before antibiotics. It was while unpacking his suitcase that his wife, Eleanor, discovered love letters from Lucy Mercer, her social secretary.

Franklin D. Roosevelt Presidential Library

Franklin D. Roosevelt Presidential Library

With the Lucy Mercer affair behind them, Eleanor and Franklin went to Europe in 1919, at the end of World War I. FDR was overseeing the return of U. S. Navy men and materiel. The couple returned aboard the USS Washington *with President Wilson who was bringing the Versailles Peace Treaty and the Covenant of the League of Nations to the Senate for ratification. Here he chats with Wilson. The president told him on the voyage that if the United States failed to enter the League of Nations, "It would break the heart of the world." It did.*

In 1920, to nearly everyone's surprise, FDR was nominated to run as candidate for vice president on the Democratic ticket. Ohio editor James M. Cox was his running mate. FDR loved the campaigning. He "whistle-stopped" across the country, meeting politicians, editors and publishers. The ticket lost badly to Warren G. Harding, but FDR had developed a nationwide network of friends, which was to be of great value later. Here he struts down Main Street in Dayton, Ohio, beside Cox.

Franklin D. Roosevelt Presidential Library

Before the 1920 political campaign began, FDR was able to spend a few weeks at Campobello with his family. Aboard his yacht, Vireo, *he works with a model sailboat. Sons James and Elliott are with him. This was to be his last visit to Campobello before his crippling attack of polio.*

Skip Cole, Roosevelt Campobello International Park

Chapter 5

"Recovered Cripple"

On August 10, 1921, FDR went for a swim in the bay behind his Campobello cottage. He climbed the hill and the stairs into the house. Telling Eleanor he thought he had "a touch of lumbago," he went up to bed. Franklin Roosevelt never walked without help again. What he thought was lumbago turned out to be paralytic polio.

The Roosevelt summer cottage was on Campobello Island. With 34 rooms, it was a great barn of a place without heat or electricity. It took Eleanor and eight servants to keep the place running. August 10, 1921, was a typical day. FDR and his children went out in their keel sloop, *Vireo*. They noticed a brush fire on an island and spent the afternoon trying to put the fire out. Bleary-eyed and soot-covered, they ran two miles across Campobello Island to a fresh water lake for a swim and then a dash into the ice cold waters of the bay. Back at the cottage, FDR said he had a touch of lumbago, and he went up the stairs to bed. He never walked again. He was thirty-nine years old.

What he had called lumbago, turned out be a severe case of polio. Polio is a viral disease that can cause permanent paralysis of the limbs, the trunk, the lungs, and, in some cases, death. It was, Eleanor said later, "a trial by fire." They were terrified the children would contract the disease. They were not sure FDR would live, nor did they know how permanent or how extensive the paralysis might be.

Campobello was, and is today, a remote place. Boston is

more than 300 miles away and Montreal is even farther. Roosevelt was desperately sick and they were far from a hospital. They were on their own.

The first thing Eleanor had to do was nurse him through the acute stage of the disease. She was with him throughout the siege, inserting catheters up his penis to drain his bladder of urine, giving enemas, moving his limbs about, hoping to alleviate the great pain that acute polio causes. She slept on a makeshift cot at the foot of his bed. Fortunately, FDR's trusted advisor Louis Howe, who had been with him ever since the New York senate days, was in the house and able to spell Eleanor with the nursing.

FDR was in the full measure of his manhood, strong and in control. Polio was a bitter, bitter blow to this golden boy, this ambitious man. Yet here he lay, unable to move his legs, not even his big toe. In the 1920s, disability was a shameful matter, like cancer or venereal disease. It was not discussed in polite society and families were expected to keep their "invalids" out of sight in a back bedroom with the blinds drawn. Roosevelt was, however, a nationally known leader of the Democratic party. He was widely touted for the presidential nomination in 1924 or 1928. Now he was paralyzed. If the extent of his paralysis became general knowledge, it was most unlikely, unthinkable really, that the voters would choose him, a crippled man, to lead the country.

Howe kept the press at bay, saying only that Roosevelt was suffering a case of influenza and was "now recovering." It was only after a month that FDR was well enough to be transferred to a New York hospital. Although he was suffering excruciating pain, Roosevelt was carried in a canvas sling-like affair, down two flights of stairs, down the steep hill to the wharf, by boat across the bay to the train station. There he was slid in his stretcher through a window into a private railroad car. Howe had misled the reporters about the time and the place of the transfer. As a result, when the press caught up with FDR, he was propped up in his railroad berth, his cigarette holder cocked at a jaunty angle, ready for an exchange of cheerful banter.

With FDR safely in the hospital, an announcement was made to the press, putting the situation in the best possible light. The *New York Times,* ran an article entitled" F.D. Roosevelt Ill of Poliomyelitis" on its front page. The story said that he was "recovering" and that "he will definitely not be crippled."

Until he contracted polio, FDR always got what he wanted. With his charm, the family money and name, the love and support of his mother, life was good and life was easy. Now none of this helped; he was in the fight of his life. He was determined to overcome the paralysis of polio. He would beat it; he would regain the use of his legs. He began the long, long, lifelong painful process of physical therapy. He essentially dropped out of public life. For seven years, he devoted the major part of every day to stretching and exercising his polio-weakened muscles. He tried all the available therapies of the time, first one and then another. He exercised in the ocean, on dry land, with braces on the parallel bars, hanging from the ceiling in a parachute harness. He tried a steam-powered tricycle his mother brought him from Europe; he used mental imaging techniques espoused by the well-known Dr. Couey, repeating to himself, over and over, "Every day in every way I am getting better and better."

Nothing seemed to help, but Roosevelt kept on trying. Raised by his mother to be a proper gentleman, reserved with his emotions, he did not complain. He was determinedly cheerful and absolutely confident he would walk again.

Roosevelt's mother thought he should retire to Hyde Park and lead the quiet, private life of a country squire. Eleanor and Howe did not agree. They believed that somehow his political career was not over, that if they or he acted as if it were, his spirit would be crushed. So they worked with FDR to keep his name before the public.

Women had just obtained the right to vote. Eleanor, shy and hesitant at first, began speaking at Democratic party events and conferences, building her own national network of women political leaders. She became a leading national figure in her own right. Working with Howe, FDR wrote articles for national magazines, issued press releases, and developed a huge correspondence, beginning with all the politicians he had met during his cross-country vice-presidential campaign.

In 1924, a friend sent him an article about a polio patient who had recovered by swimming in the warm, supposedly curative waters of Warm Springs, Georgia. Roosevelt visited the place and fell in love with it. Other polios, reading of FDR's interest, began arriving at the old ramshackle hotel, The Meriweather Inn.* Working together, FDR and the other polio created what was to become the first modern rehabilitation center. It was owned and operated by the patients, principally Roosevelt. They chose their doctors and therapists, developed their own therapies, and designed their own braces, crutches, and hand controls. Rather than exercising individual muscle groups, they taught themselves, and one another, how to live independently using the muscles they had. They learned how to be independent, and they worked hard, with the hope of resuming active and productive lives.

Warm Springs was sunny, cheerful, and fun. It was not a hospital with sick people; it was a bunch of polios who were learning to get on with their lives. Soon a campus was laid out and fully accessible buildings were built. The food was good and there were movies and parties and day-trips. There was moonshine liquor and gossip, and there were love affairs. The small town, in the pine hills of western Georgia, put in ramps and welcomed the polios with open arms. In the middle of it all, leading the band, was FDR. His upbeat and confident spirit infused the operation. It is no exaggeration to say that at Warm Springs Roosevelt and his friends developed exercises and techniques that continue to be of major benefit today to literally millions of people with disabilities around the globe.

In 1924, FDR was persuaded to nominate the New York Governor, Al Smith, for president at the Democratic convention. Roosevelt moved slowly to the podium on long leg braces and crutches, with his son behind him to catch him if he fell. The effort was substantial; sweat

---

*Although it is politically incorrect today, patients with polio at Warm Springs identified themselves proudly, as "polios." Polio survivors do so still.

poured from his forehead, and the audience held its breath. At last he reached the secure platform, gripped it and gave one of the best speeches of his life. In its glorious finish, he called for the convention to support Smith, calling him the "Happy Warrior." The delegates were silent for a minute and then leapt to their feet in cheers and applause. The ovation lasted for an hour and fifteen minutes, longer than any other in the history of the old Madison Square Garden. Roosevelt's appearance was a sensation, a triumph.

Back at Warm Springs, he was determined to learn to walk without crutches. "I'll walk into a room without scaring everyone to death. I'll stand easily in front of people so that they'll forget that I'm a cripple." After endless practice, he learned how to hold his balance, leaning on one side on the arm of one of his strong sons and using a cane as a crutch on the other. With a toddling motion, leaning from side to side, he was able to "walk," to advance by swinging one leg forward, shifting his weight, and then bringing the other leg forward. It was hard work and he was always in danger of buckling at the hips, but it worked. He was walking. Along with his sons, he taught himself how to make it appear easy, how to laugh and smile hello to people and give them the sense that everything was all right and that FDR was in full control.

The 1928 Democratic convention was in Houston. While traveling in his behalf, Eleanor wrote to FDR, "I am telling everyone you are going to Houston without crutches, so mind you stick to it." He did. Before the hushed delegates he walked to the podium with the support of no more than his cane and the arm of his son. He

again nominated Al Smith, the "Happy Warrior." Again it was a triumph. Many believed the "Happy Warrior" was Franklin D. Roosevelt. The historian Will Durant was present. He wrote that Roosevelt, ". . . a figure tall and proud even in suffering; a face of classic profile; pale with years of struggle against paralysis; a frame nervous and yet self-controlled with that tense, taut unity of spirit which lifts the . . . soul . . . a man softened and cleansed and illumined with pain. This is a civilized man."

Roosevelt so loved Warm Springs that he built a small vacation cottage on the grounds. There he would spend a week or two, once or twice a year, for the rest of his life. After he became president in 1933, the cottage was always called the Little White House. The house had a comfortably-sized living-dining room that opened out to a large deck overlooking Pine Mountain and what is now the Roosevelt National Forest. There were two small adjoining bedrooms for him and Eleanor, and a guest bedroom. The bathroom had a built-up toilet and bathtub for his use. The small kitchen had an old fashioned icebox, for which blocks of ice were delivered regularly. In contrast with the vast communications network that follows every footstep of a modern president, there was only a single telephone at the Little White House, a phone with a long cord.

After FDR became president, the wooded 900 acres of the Warm Springs Foundation were secured by the Secret Service and, during the war, by the Marine Corps. On the foundation grounds he was free to come and go as he pleased. His braces were put away and he used his little wheelchair to get around. He drove his small Ford coupe, using hand controls, and would often play bridge with the other polios or enjoy picnics on Dowdell's Knob, one of his favorite spots on Pine Mountain. He always tried to have Thanksgiving with the polio patients at Warm Springs. This was a real banquet in Georgia Hall, with turkey and all the trimmings. Of course, he sat at the head table and carved the turkey. During his presidency, Roosevelt would broadcast a Thanksgiving message to the nation during dinner.

Roosevelt loved Warm Springs. There he could be himself, relax, wear his favorite old sweater and tool about in his wheelchair. He was with his friends and fellow polios. At Warm Springs, FDR never had to worry about his paralysis or what others might be thinking about it.

Out in the world, the political world, he did have to worry about what people were thinking. He was disabled, and to most people of the day, disabled translated to crippled. Society believed that a crippled body meant a crippled mind. Roosevelt reasoned that if the public perceived him as crippled, they would base their decisions about whether to vote for him on that perception alone. Roosevelt wanted them to decide on the basis of who he was and the policies he advocated, not on whether he could stand or walk. He did not want his disability to be an issue; and so, he developed a strategy that would allow the public to ignore his disability. FDR's public appearances were carefully planned so that no one would see him being lifted into or out of a car. No one would see him being carried up steps or being pulled to a standing position on his braces. During the rest of his political life,

over the next 17 years, millions of people saw Roosevelt in parades and cavalcades, waving from the back of an open car. Millions saw him standing at a lectern, giving a speech. Millions saw him in newsreels, in *Life* magazine, and in the newspapers, working at his desk, standing at attention reviewing troops, seated before a clump of microphones in a fireside chat to the nation. But they never saw him as a disabled man. This has been called "FDR's Splendid Deception."

Franklin D. Rosevelt Presidential Library

Roosevelt spent seven years working to strengthen his polio-weakened muscles. At Warm Springs, Georgia, he joined other persons with polio to create the Georgia Warm Springs Foundation, the first modern rehabilitation center in the United States. In this photo taken in 1924 or 1925, he is shown poolside at Warm Springs. Notice the difference between his well-developed arms and shoulders and his wasted legs.

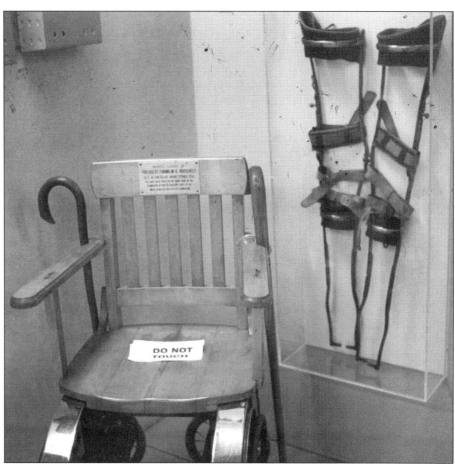

Edwin Johnson, Carl Vinson Institute of Government, University of Georgia

Here are the long leg braces, the wheelchair and two of the canes FDR used during his lengthy stays at Warm Springs. He hated wearing the braces; they were awkward and painful, but necessary. The wheels of his chair have metal fenders so that his trousers would not get mud splashed on them.

FDR exercising at the parallel bars in Warm Springs. With him are fellow polios, Fred Botts and Toi Bachelder. Botts and Roosevelt were cofounders of the rehabilitation center. Bachelder later worked as one of the President's secretaries in the White House.

In 1924, Roosevelt made a well-publicized appearance at the Democratic National Convention. With long leg braces and crutches, and with son James behind him to catch him should he fall, FDR advanced to the podium to give the "Happy Warrior" speech, one of his most famous.

Edwin Johnson, Carl Vinson Institute of Government, University of Georgia

FDR worked with the local blacksmith in designing this set of hand controls for his car. Using these controls, he was free to drive the byways of rural Georgia, stopping to talk with farmers, sharecroppers, and small town folks. This is his 1938 Ford coupe; notice the well-worn seat.

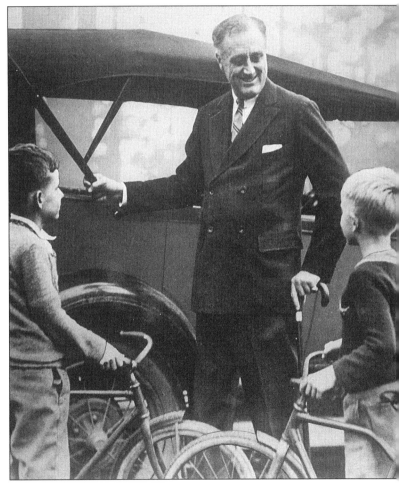

This is a carefully posed campaign photo taken at Warm Springs. Wearing his long leg braces, using his cane as a crutch and holding on to the car for balance, FDR chats with two local boys.

Franklin D. Roosevelt Presidential Library

The Roosevelts loved picnics. Here he is at Dowdells Knob on Pine Mountain, his favorite Warm Springs site. A car seat has been dragged out for him to sit on. Notice he is wearing his long leg braces over his trousers. His crutches are propped against the car.

Edwin Johnson, Carl Vinson Institute of Government, University of Georgia

FDR so loved Warm Springs, that he built a small cottage there in the pine groves. Called The Little White House during his presidency, it had an average size living-dining room, two small bedrooms with connecting bath and a grand back porch overlooking Pine Mountain. It was the only house FDR ever owned outright. Hyde Park, Hill Top, Campobello and the Manhattan townhouse were owned by his mother.

Franklin D. Roosevelt Presidential Library

Chapter *6*

Governor Roosevelt

Governor Roosevelt is sworn into office for a second term after his landslide reelection victory. Eleanor Roosevelt stands behind him, and mother, Sara Roosevelt, is behind her. Notice FDR steadies himself on the back of the armchair with his left arm, with his right arm raised to take the oath. Because of his disability, he is unable to place his hand on the Bible as is customary.

In 1928, fate came knocking. FDR took a phone call he had been avoiding for a week. It was from New York Governor Al Smith, now the Democratic candidate for president. Smith asked Roosevelt to run as the Democratic candidate for governor of New York.

It was not a good year for Democrats. The American economy had boomed under two Republican administrations. It was a "New Era," for the first time, American people could afford to buy cars, radios and phonographs, household appliances. Unemployment was low and the stock market high. Al Smith had grown up on the sidewalks of New York City. He had the urban vote on the East Coast, but in the Midwest, the South, and the West he was a stranger. He was also the first Catholic ever to run for national office. Smith had his work cut out for him. If he was to have any chance of winning the White House, he had to carry his home state of New York.

This is where FDR came in. Al was not popular upstate. Farmers, small town folks, Protestants all, saw Smith not as one of them but as a product of the city's Tammany Hall. Roosevelt, with his famous name, was from upstate. He came from an old-line, patrician Protestant family, and yet he had progressive views and had learned how to get along with Tammany Hall. With FDR's name on the ticket to appeal to upstate voters, Smith had a better chance of winning New York.

Franklin, Eleanor, and Louis Howe had planned for FDR to run for governor in 1932 and then to make his move on the White House in 1936. FDR figured that by then the boom would have lost its luster, and by then he would be able to walk using only a cane. Smith begged him to run for governor, but FDR said no. Smith pleaded with him, arguing that Roosevelt would not have to campaign, would make only a few speeches, and that all the costs would be covered. As governor, FDR could stay in Warm Springs and turn the day-to-day operations over to the lieutenant governor. Roosevelt could be the figurehead and Smith and his men would handle the politics. FDR still said no.

Smith then asked FDR what he would do if the New York convention drafted him—nominated him without his express consent. FDR said he didn't know. With this, Smith had Roosevelt's name placed before the convention and FDR was nominated for governor by acclamation.

Roosevelt accepted the nomination. Eleanor telegraphed him, "Regret that you had to accept but know that you felt it obligatory." The newspapers praised his candidacy; even Republican newspapers called FDR, "a fair-minded and cultivated man." Although Roosevelt referred to himself as a "recovered cripple," some papers were not so sure. The *New York Post* said, "There is something both pathetic and pitiless about the drafting of Franklin D. Roosevelt . . . even [his] own friends, out of love for him, will hesitate to vote for him now." Smith countered this by saying, famously, "A governor does not have to be an acrobat."

FDR hit the issue dead on:

I am amazed that people are being told 'to vote against me to prevent my sacrificing myself.' I do not feel that appeals to personal friendship should form any part of a plea to the electorate. But if I did, my own plea would be, 'Not only do I want my friends to vote for me, but if they are my real friends, I ask them to get as many other people to vote for me as possible.'

I trust this statement will eliminate this particular piece of nonsense from the campaign from the very beginning."

On the campaign's very first stop, there was a passel of reporters, photographers and newsreel cameras waiting on the curb. As Roosevelt was being lifted out of the car to a standing position, he waved to the cameramen, "No movies of me getting out of the machine, boys!" The men put down their cameras. Throughout the remaining 17 years of his political life, no photo showing FDR's disability was ever printed in the press nor was it mentioned in news stories.

FDR fooled everybody. He launched a vigorous campaign and traveled by open touring car from one end of the state to the other. He spoke from morning to night, in small towns and big cities. He exhausted the reporters covering his campaign. He spoke of farm issues and social problems, and at the end of every speech he would recite his schedule: "Herkimer, Fonda, Gloversville, Amsterdam . . . and then for good measure, we just dropped into Schenectady and spoke there early in the evening and now here we are in Troy." He would pause and then add, "Too bad about this unfortunate sick man, isn't it?" The crowd would roar with laughter.

On election day, Al Smith lost to Herbert Hoover by a landslide. He even lost New York. To everyone's astonishment, Roosevelt won the race for governor. FDR had been out of public life for seven years. He had not held elective office in 15 years. And yet, in a Republican landslide, Democrat Franklin Roosevelt had won This election made him at once a leading figure in the party and a prospective candidate for president in 1932.

✳ ✳ ✳

The Roosevelts took over the big old governor's mansion in Albany with gusto. Life in the mansion was a circus. There were bedrooms for Franklin, Eleanor, the four boys—now teenagers, for Louis Howe, Missy LeHand, and mother Sara. Daughter Anna was married, but the boys were in and out of the house with their prep school and college buddies. They played loud music on their phonographs and got into teen age scrapes with regularity. The New York press took delight in covering their wild parties and speeding tickets.

There were always house guests: cousins, friends, and a variety of others: politicians from all over the country, professors with ideas, reporters, writers, social workers, celebrities, business moguls, lawyers, Indian chiefs, and teenagers. You never knew who would be at the dinner table. Although Franklin had limited mobility, he wanted to keep abreast of what was happening. And so, both Eleanor and Franklin made conscious efforts to bring significant people of all kinds to meet and talk with the governor. This practice was good politics, but it was more than that. The Roosevelts genuinely liked people and were concerned with social issues and policies. At their dinner table they heard new ideas and differing points of view on controversial issues. The Roosevelts learned

from their guests, and many of them became friends.

Eleanor acted as first lady four days a week and taught at the Todhunter Girls School in Manhattan three days a week. She was a co-owner of this school, which she hoped to model after Allenwood, Mme. Souvestre's school in England that had meant so much to her. She and two of her close friends also established a small factory on the grounds of the Roosevelt estate to employ out-of-work craftsmen who turned out fine handmade reproductions of colonial antiques. As if this was not enough, Eleanor was the leading woman in the New York Democratic party and a powerhouse on the National Democratic Committee. She was building a nation-wide network of women in politics. As a national figure, she gave speeches and wrote a stream of articles and op-ed pieces on women's issues and social policy. Eleanor was also a mother and a wife. In the face of all this she remained calm, never seemed to be flustered, and was always willing to listen.

As governor, FDR developed a daily routine he was to take with him to the White House. The mansion was ramped for his wheelchair and an elevator installed. Rich friends built an indoor swimming pool for his use. FDR would awaken around eight, read the papers, and have his breakfast in bed. Still in bed, he would take phone calls and dictate correspondence to Missy, who had an adjoining bedroom. Around ten, he would go in his wheelchair to his office in the capitol. Transferred to the chair behind his desk, his wheelchair out of sight, he would meet and have appointments. Usually he would take his lunch at his desk, often with legislators or reporters. If the legislature was in session, he might work long into the night, but usually he would return to the mansion in midafternoon for a massage, a rubdown, and a rest.

Gus Gennerich, a New York City policeman who had been detailed to protect FDR during the campaign, took leave from the force and joined the governor's staff. Earl Miller, a state trooper, became FDR's bodyguard. Both Gennerich and Miller regularly ate at table with the Roosevelts. Like Howe and Missy LeHand, they became part of the Roosevelt family. FDR no longer had to worry about finding the accessible way to do things. Gennerich and Miller were always available to lift him in and out of the car, to pull his wheelchair up and down steps, and to provide a strong arm when FDR was up on his braces.

Former Governor Al Smith thought that FDR was an upper-class lightweight. Smith, a product of the Tammany machine, had planned on being the power behind the throne, handling the nuts and bolts of politics and policy. It didn't work out that way. FDR was governor in every sense from the very start. Smith told the new governor that he was preparing a message and program for FDR to send to the legislature. "Too late," said FDR, "I have already written my own." Roosevelt said later to Frances Perkins, "I didn't feel able to make this campaign for governor, but I made it. I didn't feel that I was sufficiently recovered to undertake the duties of governor of New York, but here I am. After Al said that to me, I thought about myself and I realized that I've got to be governor of the state of New York and I have got to be it myself." And so he was.

As Governor, he fought to regulate the private utilities to ensure fair electricity and water rates; he reformed the state's judicial and penal systems; he supported environmental conservation; and he established a strong program for the advancement of the rights of labor. As part of his very first message to the legislature, he made a particularly revolutionary proposal. He said, "I conceive it to be the duty of the state to give the same care to removing the physical handicaps of its citizens as it now gives to their mental development. Universal education of the mind is, after all, a modern conception. We have reached the time now when we must recognize the same obligation of the state to restore to useful activity those children and adults who have the misfortune to be crippled . . . As a matter of good business, it would pay the state to help in restoring these cripples to useful citizenship." Alas, this worthy proposal was never enacted.

The Roosevelts were open with the press. FDR's fight with the private utility giants received nationwide attention. Speculation about his presidential ambitions mounted. Both he and Eleanor traveled widely across the state. They took a well-publicized vacation aboard a houseboat, cruising down the Erie Canal, all across New York. They stopped and talked with folks along the way, gave speeches in small towns, and everywhere they went they spread a sort of Roosevelt magic. FDR made use of the radio, a communication device only recently installed in American homes. As governor, he gave monthly radio reports to the people of New York. He spoke in a comfortable, conversational way, far removed from the snooty high society tones of his early speeches when he had first entered politics. Voters warmed to his voice and the broadcasts were a big success.

FDR was elected governor of New York in 1928, by a slim margin. When he ran for reelection in 1930, he won by a huge majority. The Oklahoma cowboy comic Will Rogers was not joking when he remarked, "The Democrats nominated their president yesterday." In the same election, the Democrats took control of the U.S. House of Representatives and almost took the U.S. Senate. Politicians saw the country going Democratic in 1932.

This national swing to the Democrats was caused, in part, by the great stock market crash that began on Black Thursday—October 24, 1929. Over the months, the market fell farther and faster than ever before or since. The market as measured by the Dow Jones industrial average went from a high of 387.17 to a low of 41.22 in 1932. At a time when the federal budget ran at $300 million and hamburgers cost a nickel, stocks dropped an estimated $50 billion in value. As an example, a share of General Electric went from $403 to $8.50. Fortunes were lost, loans were called, businesses failed, factories closed, and farm prices plummeted. The nation began its slide into the Great Depression, a crisis as great and as dangerous to American democracy as the Civil War.

As the 1930s began, more and more people were out of work. More and more homes and farms were repossessed. Whole families faced starvation on the streets. Without leadership, assistance or action from Washington, D.C., Roosevelt acted on his own. He believed that government should and can, "act to protect its citizens from disaster." Within the state of New York, he increased public works programs that put people back to work and established a program that provided cash relief to the needy. It was not much, but it was enough to ward off hunger. FDR also pushed for state-sponsored unemployment compensation and old age benefits.

New York was leading the nation in its response to the Depression. This response generated much attention from the press and from party officials looking for a presidential candidate for 1932. The world seemed to beat a path to FDR's door at Hyde Park. He conferred with mayors, governors, congressmen, party bosses. They were invited to lunches and dinners. The aristocratic Sara, immensely proud of her son, raised nary a peep as she presided over a motley crew of guests at her dinner table—although, she was once overheard to say of Huey Long, the swaggering "Kingfish" of Louisiana, "Who is that dreadful person?"

FDR's campaign for the Democratic nomination as president switched into high gear. With Louis Howe's help, FDR carried on an endless correspondence, writing letters to people he had met in the 1920 campaign, to people who had written to him throughout the 1920s, and to all those he thought might support him. He hired Jim Farley, a remarkable political operative, to travel the country talking up FDR's candidacy and downplaying Roosevelt's disability.

Even so, Roosevelt's health became the subject of a nationwide whispering campaign. As *Time* magazine reported, quoting one observer, "This candidate, while qualified mentally to be president, is utterly unfit physically." Farley reported that he was asked about FDR's disability at every stop on his trip west. A vicious anonymous flyer was sent to convention delegates claiming that the disability was caused by end-stage syphilis. To counter this kind of talk, Roosevelt announced that he was taking out half a million dollars worth of life insurance. After a thorough physical examination, the insurance doctors reported to the press that they had given the governor a clean bill of health—all in all, "an excellent physical specimen."

To further emphasize FDR's good health and stamina, the Roosevelt camp challenged a well-known Republican writer to investigate FDR's fitness for office and to report on it in *Liberty,* a popular magazine of the day. The challenge was a bit of a cooked up affair. The writer was a friend of Franklin's cousin Teddy, and he had actually ghostwritten some pieces for FDR. In the course of his investigation, the writer talked with doctors, friends and coworkers. He followed FDR throughout a full day's work. When the article was published, its summary was, "In so far as I have observed, I have come to the conclusion that he seemed to be able to take more punishment than a many a man ten years younger. Merely his legs were not much good to him."

FDR assembled a group of experts on economic, social, domestic, and foreign issues. This group came to be called the "brain trust." Many a night around the fire at Hyde Park, he would ask them questions, probe their minds, and debate with them. Gradually he put together his understanding of the causes of the Depression and the policies to be taken to return the nation to prosperity.

Going into the nominating convention, the Roosevelt forces did not have the two-thirds of the delegates needed for nomination. Only after much bargaining and much dealing between FDR's camp and the other branches of the Democratic party (the regional progressives, the urban machines) was the nomination clinched on the fourth ballot. It was the tradition that the presidential nominee stayed away from the convention. Supposedly, his friends would put forward his name to the party and work for his nomination, while the man himself remained above the fray. Roosevelt broke with this tradition in a spectacular way. He announced he would accept the nomination in a speech, in person, at the convention.

Not only would he appear in person, he would fly to the convention! This was electrifying news. Back then, only the daring and foolhardy risked air travel. Nevertheless, FDR and his family boarded a corrugated Ford Trimotor plane and flew to the convention in Chicago. They encountered strong and rough head winds, the plane had to land twice to refuel, and his sons became airsick. On arrival, the sons had a terrible time straightening FDR's braces and getting him into a standing position at the doorway to face the horde of press photographers and reporters that rushed from the gate.

Many, many thousands of citizens turned out to line his route as he drove in an open car to the convention. After a tumultuous welcome at Chicago Stadium, Roosevelt addressed the convention while the entire nation listened on the radio. "I pledge you, I pledge myself, to a new deal for the American people . . . Give me your help, not to win votes alone, but to win in this crusade to restore America back to its own people."

Deafening cheers filled the stadium and rang out across America. The New Deal had been born and the band struck up the tune that has become the anthem of the Democratic party, "Happy Days Are Here Again!"

Franklin D. Rossevelt Presidential Library

The governor greets guests from a seated position at his inaugural ball. Eleanor, now first lady of New York, stands beside him in the receiving line. The unknown guest is dressed in the height of 1929 fashion: marcelled hair, short skirt, long waist and pearls.

Franklin D. Rossevelt Presidential Library

Roosevelt inspects the New York National Guard at Camp Trumbull. He reviews the troops from a seated position in the back of an open car. He used this method for the rest of his political career while visiting army or navy sites, factories, parks, and rallies. In addressing small crowds, he would remain seated in the car.

Even though teaching school part-time, writing articles and speaking across the country, Eleanor Roosevelt was an active first lady. Here she is visiting a shop in the Empire State Building operated by the New York State Commission for the Blind. With her are Helen Keller, a famous writer and social activist who was both blind and deaf, and Miss Byrnes, a blind salesperson.

Franklin D. Rossevelt Presidential Library

Franklin D. Roosevelt Presidential Library

Although an active governor, Roosevelt was able to slip away several times a year to Warm Springs, Georgia, for intensive physical therapy and relaxation. Here he is shown fishing on the Flint River, one of his favorite pastimes. The name of the puppy in his arms is unknown.

Franklin D. Rossevelt Presidential Library

The governor meets Martha Hill, an 103-year-old Onondaga Indian at the State Fair.

As governor, Roosevelt was expected to meet with various delegations and groups.

The governor is presented with an archery set by the Dutchess County Boy Scout Council.

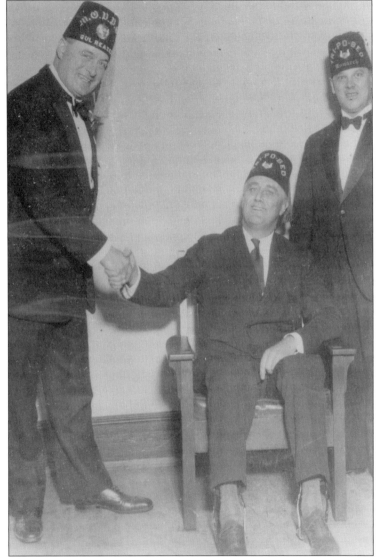

The governor is made a Masonic "Prophet at Sight" in the Tri-Bo-Ped Grotto.

The governor is initiated into the Improved Order of Red Men in this photo.

Franklin D. Roosevelt Presidential Library

Franklin and Eleanor and secretary Missy LeHand poolside at Eleanor's cottage, Val Kill, on the grounds of their Hyde Park estate. Roosevelt loved swimming because his weakened leg muscles could function in the buoyant water.

Franklin D. Rossevelt Presidential Library

As part of his run for the Democratic nomination for President, FDR met and cemented his friendship with political leaders across the country. In this photo he meets with Colonel Edmund House, a member of the party Old Guard, Mayor James Curley, the boss of Boston politics, and Senator David Walsh (D-Montana), a leader on Capitol Hill. FDR, using his cane and long leg braces to form a tripod, leans against the door frame to keep his balance.

Franklin D. Rossevelt Presidential Library

After a harrowing flight in a small Ford Trimotor plane, FDR arrives in Chicago to give his acceptance speech at the 1932 Democratic convention. His arrival caused a sensation. He was the first candidate ever to appear in person before a convention. Sons James and John had a most difficult time getting Roosevelt and his braces out of the plane into a standing position.

Franklin D. Roosevelt Presidential Library

Franklin D. Roosevelt Presidential Library

Chapter *7*

"Dr. New Deal"

Years of drought coupled with strong winds caused massive dust storms, called "Black Blizzards," to blow across the Great Plains. This photo of an approaching storm was taken by a farmer living in Rolla, Kansas. He sent it to FDR with a note that reads:

05/06/35

Dear Mr. President,

Darkness when it hit us. Picture taken from water tower one hundred feet high.

Yours Truly, Chas. P. Williams.

In the 1932 presidential election, FDR swamped President Hoover, winning 472 electoral votes to Hoover's 59. Both houses of Congress gained large Democratic majorities. Roosevelt had a clear mandate to lead—but where? And how? He had the momentum, he had the nation behind him. Even the conservative *Wall Street Journal* said in an editorial "it is time to make sacrifices to a common necessity and to accept realities." In politics, timing is all. This was the time to act and, over his first Hundred Days in the White House, FDR acted.

FDR's philosophy of government was pragmatic, he sought solutions to problems, and the problems he faced in 1933 threatened the future of American democracy. His job was to save the American system. He faced the Great Depression as he had faced polio: he used whatever therapies were available to meet immediate problems. He said "The country needs, and unless I mistake its temper, the country demands bold, persistent experimentation. It is common sense to take a method and try it. If it fails, admit it frankly and try another. But above all, try something."

Roosevelt was sworn into office on Saturday, March 4, 1933.

That night, there were inaugural balls all over town. Eleanor attended on behalf of the president, but he remained in the White House conferring with Treasury officials on the crisis in banking. Over the previous two weeks, the crisis had come to a head; even stable banks were failing as depositors rushed to withdraw their savings. On Sunday, March 5, Roosevelt proclaimed a "Bank Holiday," thereby closing every bank in America for three days. If people did not have cash, they had to rely on barter or IOUs. Even Eleanor was caught short. She had to scrape together the cash needed for her sons to return to school.

FDR held his first press conference on Monday, March 6. Unlike previous presidents, he took any and all questions, answering frankly when he could, cagily when he could not. Roosevelt continued this policy throughout his four terms in office, holding two press conferences a week on average. He called a special session of Congress to meet on March 8, 1933, and sent them the Emergency Banking Act. This measure called for the federal government to provide cash backing to rescue sound banks in need, to prevent the hoarding and export of gold, and to provide federal oversight to ensure sound banking practices. The president also went on the air with his first "Fireside Chat," an informal talk from the White House study to the American people. He carefully explained the banking crisis—what had caused it, and what his administration was doing about it. FDR's message was so clear, said cowboy wit Will Rogers, that he "made everyone understand it, even the bankers."

This revolutionary proposal, the Emergency Banking Act, was sent to Capitol Hill on March 9, 1933. It was passed by virtually unanimous consent the same day and signed into law that night. As the House Republican leader said when urging his side of the aisle to support the bill, a bill that members had not read, "The house is burning down and the president of the United States says this is the way to put out the fire." This banking measure, plus federal government insurance for all federally regulated bank accounts, added a month later, guaranteed that America's banking system was safe and secure, as it has been ever since.

When the banks reopened, people began to return their deposits to the banks; there were no more runs on the banks and the crisis was over. The success of President Roosevelt's decisive action greatly increased the faith of the America people in their new leader.

In the first Hundred Days of his term, the Congress approved a series of proposals that constituted no less than a peaceful revolution in the duties and responsibilities of the government of the United States. To achieve this revolution, Roosevelt skillfully used all the powers of the president. He had the bills he wanted drafted in the executive department. He met one-on-one with members of Congress to persuade them to his side. He freely used the politics of horse swapping and patronage to get votes. He kept pressure on the Congress and used the veto and the threat of veto to deflect amendments he did not like. Through the press and his fireside chats, he went over the head of the Congress to build support for his programs.

No president had ever been so effective, no Congress ever so productive. Within these 100 days, FDR sent 15 messages to Congress containing proposals, and the Congress passed 15 major pieces of legislation incorporating these proposals into law. Here is the record:

• **MARCH 10, 1933** Economy: FDR asked the Congress to reduce government expenditures by roughly 13 percent. Civil servants' salaries were reduced and some government employees were fired. Veterans' pensions were cut by 25 percent. This was part of an attempt to hold down the federal budget. The attempt failed. Roosevelt's administration was forced to go billions of dollars in debt in its efforts to put men back to work and to get factories back in production.

• **MARCH 16, 1933** Farm relief: FDR asked for federal backing on loans to farmers, subsidies for those who reduced the size of their crops to bring their output into balance with demand, and relief of bank pressure on farm mortgages. The Agricultural Assistance Act and the Emergency Farm Mortgage Act became law, but federal planning for agriculture (crop allotments and subsidies) has remained controversial to this day.

• **MARCH 21, 1933** Conservation: FDR asked for, and Congress approved, the creation of the Civilian Conservation Corps (CCC). Within several months, more that 250,000 young men were at work in the national parks and forests, building lodges, maintaining roads, planting trees, and fighting forest fires. They lived in camps provided by the army, received healthy meals, medical care, and for many, the first visit ever to a dentist. They were paid $33 a month and allowed to send $22 of it back to their families. Many a hungry sharecropper family eked out its existence during those bitter months on the money their sons sent them. Illiterate CCC boys were taught to read, and those who were able to read received college preparation. More

than 2.5 million men served in the CCC. When the nation mobilized for World War II, the CCC boys became the backbone of the American army.

• **MARCH 21, 1933** Direct unemployment relief: FDR asked for and received $500 million, larger than the federal budget of the previous year. Grants were made to states and localities to provide immediate relief to out-of-work men and their families. In his first two hours on the job, program director Harry Hopkins dispensed $5 million to the states. "Money Flies" cried the *Washington Post*. By midyear, this program had evolved into the Civil Works Administration (CWA), which put unemployed workers back to work on federally financed projects. At its height, CWA employed more than 4 million persons working on some 400,000 sites, including schools, roads, parks, sewers. Hopkins funded any worthwhile activity he could think up. CWA did much to restore the dignity of blue-collar workers and their families. Even Republican Alf Landon, who would run against FDR in 1936, wrote the president, calling CWA, "one of the soundest and most constructive programs of your administration."

• **MARCH 29, 1933** Regulation of stock markets: The Truth in Securities Act and, later, the Securities and Exchange Act, authorized regulation of the issuance of company stock, of the purchase and sale of stock, and of limits on the buying of stock on credit. It required all companies with public stock holdings to provide full and accurate information on their operations to federal examiners.

• **APRIL 10, 1933** Tennessee Valley Authority: This act called upon the government to develop the economy of a huge river basin in the south central region of America.

TVA built dams, power plants, locks for river transport, flood control projects, and fertilizer factories. TVA reclaimed burnt-out farm lands, reforested millions of acres, and brought cheap electric power to millions of people. It is the most successful such project in the world.

• MAY 4, 1933 Home mortgages: At FDR's request, Congress gave the president the authority to save mortgaged homes from foreclosure by banks and holding companies. At that time, homeowners were losing their houses at the rate of a thousand a day. Under the program, interest payments on home mortgages were renegotiated at lower rates and payments were delayed.

• JUNE 16, 1933 Regulation of the economy: The National Industrial Recovery Act (NIRA), the most controversial of the New Deal programs, authorized the negotiation and application of industry-wide codes of operation regarding pricing, production, wages, work conditions and hours. If this part of the NIRA had not been struck down as unconstitutional by the U. S. Supreme Court, the United States might have turned into a cartel-run economy.

The second part of NIRA set up the Public Works Administration (PWA). This authorized a huge program of public works projects across the country to put more people back to work. By the time it ended in World War II, many billions had been spent on dams, flood control projects, rural electrification, slum clearance, student scholarships, and construction of schools, post offices, and courthouses.

New Deal projects were not just for blue-collar workers. Artists, writers, and actors, were put to work. As many as 15,000 actors, designers, and directors were put on the payroll, creating plays and musicals in cities and towns across the country. The Federal Theater Project played to an audience of over four million over a four year period. Some of America's finest artists—including Thomas Hart Benson, George Bellows, Reginald Marsh, William de Kooning, and Jackson Pollock—survived the Depression thanks to this program.. The paintings, murals, and sculptures created for this New Deal program convey the energy, determination, and pride of those years. These works are now worth many millions of dollars.

The Federal Writers Project helped such great authors as Richard Wright and John Cheever to weather the Depression. Scholars researched U. S. history documents, wrote regional histories, and created the WPA state guides, the best American guidebooks ever. Musicians recorded the origins of the blues, jazz, and spirituals. Photographers such as Walker Evans and Dorothea Lange, recorded for all time the America of the 1930s: skyscrapers, breadlines, great dams and power projects, Main Street on Saturday afternoon.

The National Youth Administration (NYA) found jobs for a million and a half high school students and more than 600,000 college students so they could finish their education. NYA also found employment for more than 4 million young people who had dropped out of school and were jobless.

✳ ✳ ✳

Almost overnight, Washington, D. C., a sleepy southern town, became America's happening place. Thousands of smart, ambitious, and idealistic young lawyers, public administrators, welfare workers came to Washington to build their careers in public service. They were the New Dealers. They organized and administered the myriad of confusing new alphabet soup agencies: AAA, CCC, SEC, TVA, PWA, WPA, NRA, NYA, FWP. It was an exciting time. A genuine, oftentimes naive, optimism swirled through the usual cynical politics of the capitol city.

Roosevelt's New Deal changed the very face of America, the way people do business, the responsibilities of government. Everything was changed by the New Deal. Americans were swept up in a common purpose, united as a national community. They developed a shared sense of responsibility for the well-being of all, a shared determination that by working together, America could defeat the Great Depression.

The Great Depression, which had begun with bank failures in central Europe, spread worldwide. Franklin Roosevelt's response to the crisis was watched with great interest by the leaders of the world. In England, Winston Churchill, certainly no radical, congratulated FDR for his "noble and heroic sanity." British economist Lord Keynes, who *was* radical, said "President Roosevelt is magnificently right." Even in Germany, the new fuhrer, Adolph Hitler remarked, "I have sympathy with President Roosevelt because he marches straight to his objective over Congress, over lobbies, over bureaucracies."

This was precisely what began to worry FDR's critics. Was Roosevelt taking on the powers of a Fascist or Communist dictator? A small but loud minority began to

think so. FDR had such public support, they feared he could simply override the restraints provided in the Constitution to check the seizure of power by any one of the three branches of government: the Congress, the Supreme Court, or the president. Opposition built quickly. The FDR honeymoon when all federal branches united in support of his emergency measures, did not last long. Only the first of Roosevelt's bills passed quickly without congressional scrutiny or criticism. Increasingly over the Hundred Days, the Congress balked. Congressional committees studied the administration's proposals and came up with amendments and additions. Republican Members opposed some of these proposals, amended or not, and those measures barely obtained passage.

Hard times produce radical leaders with radical proposals. Such leaders arose on both the political left and right. On the left there was Huey Long, the "Kingfish" of Louisiana. Huey was a rapscallion, smart as a whip, who had risen from poverty to become the absolute boss of Louisiana politics. Once when he was raising money for his campaigns, he told a group of businessman, " Those who come in with me now will get big pieces of pie. Those who come in with me later will get smaller pieces of pie. Those who don't come in at all will get good government." Long began a national campaign designed to place him to run for president in 1936. In his "Share the Wealth" program Long proposed breaking up all private fortunes above a given amount, and using the money so that every family would have a home, a car, and a radio, with pensions for the old and college scholarships for the young. The workweek would be shortened, a minimum wage would be set, and all workers would receive immediate bonuses. By 1935, Long had 27,000 "Share the Wealth" clubs across the country and a mailing list of 7.5 million.

The congressional elections of 1934 demonstrated strong public support for President Roosevelt and his policies. It is axiomatic that the party in control of the White House loses seats in the midterm elections. But in 1934, the Democrats gained seats—they now controlled three quarters of the House of Representatives and two thirds of the Senate. Backed by such majorities, FDR now pushed for a reform package that has been called, the Second Hundred Days. Passage of these measures was by no means as easy as it had been in 1933. Conservative southern Democrats, congressmen backed by mining and industrial interests, joined with Republicans to force major concessions from the White House. Nevertheless, a huge $5 billion dollars was approved to put men to work and prime the economy. Social Security was approved, as was the Fair Labor Standards Act, and the Public Utility Holding Act. To the lasting shock of the wealthy, Roosevelt called for a "public policy of encouraging a wider distribution of wealth." He asked for, and received, authority from the Congress to raise the taxes of the rich, from 59 percent to 75 percent in the highest income bracket.

This period was the apogee of the New Deal reforms. In but three years, America had undergone a peaceful revolution. The nation as we know it today—with workers' rights, unemployment insurance, a social safety net, guaranteed bank deposits and mortgages, protected investments, and regulated markets—these reforms and many more were created by the New Deal of President Roosevelt.

Unemployment was down, the stock market was up, and crop prices had stabilized. The panic and fear of 1932 receded. But opposition to what some called the high-handed behavior of FDR began to develop. Opposition came from both left and right.

On the right, the Liberty League, funded by the du Ponts and made up of Al Smith and other conservative Democrats, was dedicated to the sanctity of private capital. These opponents were furious over government interference, through taxes and regulation, with their freedom to make money. The League railed against "That Man in the White House." They were joined soon enough by bankers, executives and conservative newspaper publishers. Roosevelt was a dictator, they said, and he was riding roughshod over the checks and balance of our democratic system. With his socialist, expensive public welfare programs, the president was spending the nation into bankruptcy. "There can be only one capitol," shouted an old, embittered Al Smith,"Washington or Moscow!"

The left was just as angry and even more threatening. Father Coughlin was a Roman Catholic priest who had a weekly national broadcast. He had a fine radio voice and a charming personality. His program of political and social commentary was the most popular show on the air. He received more letters than anyone else in the country, even President Roosevelt. His popularity gave him considerable political power, particularly in the urban northeast. Coughlin was a quirky, irascible guy. He was with FDR at the beginning of the New Deal, but soon broke with him and developed a bitter, anti-Semitic, anti-immigrant isolation policy of his own. He wanted the United States to adopt a system of "social justice" modeled on dictator Mussolini's Italy. Coughlin believed the Depression was caused by evil international Jewish bankers, who were, he said, manipulating gold. There must be a "religious crusade against the pagan god of gold." Salvation was to be found in silver which he called the "gentile" or non-Jewish metal. Roosevelt, he cried, was the tool of the banker devils. The New Deal had become the "Pagan Deal." "Roosevelt was the great betrayer and liar," shouted Coughlin. He was "Franklin Double Crossing Roosevelt!"

✳ ✳ ✳

The Roosevelts moved into the White House in 1933 as if they had always lived there. The style was Roosevelt informal. You never knew who you might meet or what was going on at the White House. The house was always full. There were endless teas, lunches, dinners for visitors, and many overnight guests. According to biographer Ted Morgan, it was always *Hellzapoppin* (the title of a popular play of the time) at the White House. The Roosevelt family became celebrities and their every move was covered by the press.

The First Lady furnished the second-floor family quarters with old and comfortable furniture. FDR's bedroom, office and study were hung with engravings of American clipper ships. His ship models were placed about the Oval Office. His big desk became filled with model donkeys and other gewgaws sent to him from around the country.

Eleanor used her bedroom as an office and slept in the small attached dressing room. The ailing Louis Howe took

a corner bedroom; Missy lived up on the third floor. Daughter Anna, now separated from her husband, moved in with her two small children. Roosevelt's sons had various bedrooms from time to time. The president's confidential advisor Harry Hopkins, brought his daughter Diana, and later his new wife Louise, to live with the Roosevelts. House guests were visiting family members, heads of state, old friends, musicians, magicians, movie stars, polio patients, women's rights advocates. You name it, they all stayed at the White House.

One day, while driving alone, Eleanor stopped to pick up a hitchhiker, an out-of-work teen age boy who had no place to sleep. She took him to the White House for the night. She arranged a job for him with the National Youth Administration. When he got married, she attended the wedding, served as godmother for his child, and kept in touch with him throughout his life.

Another time, Eleanor received a letter from a New York state middle school teacher who was bringing her class to Washington to visit the historic sites. The teacher wrote that one of her students used a wheelchair because he had been disabled by polio. Would the first lady know of an accessible hotel where he might stay? Let him stay at the White House, the first lady replied. And he did, breakfasting with the president in his bedroom every morning. At the boy's last breakfast, FDR pointed to his closet, and told the boy to take home a necktie as a souvenir.

Even heads of state, on official visits, were treated with the same Roosevelt warmth and informality. This treatment did not always work out well. During World War II, Mme. Chiang Kai-Shek, the wife of the generalissimo, ruler of Nationalist China, came to visit. To the Roosevelts' surprise, she brought with her two nurses, her brother, his wife and their grown daughter. The daughter dressed like a man, confusing everyone in the household. Mme. Chiang also brought with her a large supply of silk bed sheets which she insisted be changed and washed every time she lay down, and she lay down often. Madame was small, charming and beautiful. She could charm a snake out of a tree, but she was tough as nails and rude to anyone she considered an inferior, which was just about everybody. She stayed on and on, using the White House as a hotel. The Roosevelts had a hard time getting her to leave.

The king and queen of Great Britain came to stay on a historic state visit in June of 1939. After the formal ceremonies, receptions and dinners, Eleanor and Franklin took the young couple to Hyde Park for a family weekend. Over Sara Roosevelt's objections, the Secret Service insisted that White House staff be used in her house during the royal visit. At dinner with just the family and the king and queen, the overloaded serving table crashed to the floor. In the stunned silence that followed, daughter Anna spoke out, "I hope that wasn't my china!" As if this was not enough, after dinner, the butler stumbled on the wheelchair ramp leading into the library, falling flat with a great crash, spilling tray, ice, ginger ale and all. The rest of her life, FDR's mother would say, "None of this would have happened, if my butler had been used."

The Roosevelts were always on the go. When the president traveled, he used a private Pullman car and with other cars full of staff and reporters, toured the country by private train. In 1942, the Pullman Company built him an armored car with 3 inch thick bulletproof glass windows, The *Ferdinand Magellan*. The car was more than three times as heavy as an ordinary passenger railroad car. Roosevelt liked to travel at 35 miles an hour so as to see the countryside, but at night while FDR was sleeping, the engineer made up for lost time. The *Magellan* had a plush observation lounge, a dining room that seated eight, and a presidential suite with bedrooms for the first lady and FDR with a connecting bathroom large enough to provide full access for his wheelchair. An elevator was installed on the observation platform for FDR's use in getting on and off the train. Over the remaining years of his presidency, he traveled more than 50,0000 miles in the *Magellan*.

Eleanor, acting as FDR's eyes and ears, traveled alone or with her secretary, Malvina Thompson. In Washington and Hyde Park, she drove to appointments herself in her own car. She refused Secret Service protection, thus really exasperating the Service. She finally did agree to take shooting lessons and, sometimes at the insistence of the Secret Service, she carried a small pistol in her purse. During one dangerous encounter, she actually had the pistol out and on the seat beside her as she drove. Over the many years of her travels, meeting and speaking to millions, she said she had never had an "unpleasant incident," although, she added, "I have had a tail pulled off my fur scarf as a souvenir, but nothing worse than that has ever happened."

Eleanor Roosevelt traveled many hundreds of thousands of miles, back and forth across the nation in peacetime, and to Europe and the South Pacific in wartime. In her travels, Eleanor Roosevelt inspected CCC camps, public works projects, hospitals, and social service programs.

These visits were not just walk-throughs with a bouquet of roses in her arms. She would taste the food, inspect the closets, talk with employees, and, in hospitals, have a word with every patient. When she found things that needed attention she would bring them to the attention of the president or to the head of the department involved. And she would follow up, to make sure the problems were resolved.

Twice a year she made lecture tours of two or three weeks duration across the country. These lectures were always well attended. She met the press wherever she went, and had a weekly White House press conference for women reporters. Throughout her White House years, she wrote a daily newspaper column, "My Day," that was at one time the most widely syndicated column in the country. She had a weekly national radio show and, for years, wrote a monthly column in *Ladies Home Journal*. In addition to all these activities, she was a gracious hostess. In the year 1939, she had 323 overnight guests at the White House; 4,729 guests for lunch or dinner; and 9,211 for tea. In her first nine months as first lady, she received and answered some 300,000 letters.

Eleanor Roosevelt became the best known and most popular first lady in history. She was also, by far, the most powerful woman U. S. history. She had strong liberal opinions that she expressed with force and clarity. She was in favor of women's rights and workers rights, and she opposed segregation of any kind. She gave her strong support to New Deal programs and pushed for more. Because she always had the President's ear, politicians and officials listened to her. She was hated greatly in the still segregated South and widely ridiculed in the right-wing press. Nothing fazed her. A Gallup Poll showed that two-thirds of Americans supported her work, while one-third violently opposed it.

Eleanor and Franklin Roosevelt were a team. Without her, there would have been no New Deal. She was the idealist; he was the politician. She knew what should be done; he knew how to go about getting it done. Sometimes she differed with him and caused him political embarrassment. Nevertheless he told her, "You go right ahead and stand for what you think is right . . . I can always say I can't do a thing with you!"

Franklin D. Roosevelt Presidential Library

Here a family in Appalachia share their Christmas dinner. They live in a small one-room cabin. Note the iron bedstead on the left, the wood stove on the right.

Franklin D. Roosevelt Presidential Library

Franklin D. Roosevelt Presidential Library

Times were so bad in the 1930s that farmers lost their farms, farming equipment, houses, furniture, everything. They barely made pennies on the dollar at auctions and yard sales. No one else had money either. Many farm families packed what few possessions they had into their model-T Fords and headed toward California, hoping to make a better life there.

Times were hard in California too, and jobs were few. Living conditions were no better than they had been in the Plains states. Here a family of "Oakies" (Oklahoma farmers who had given up their homes and gone to California looking for work) live in a makeshift tent city.

Franklin D. Rossevelt Presidential Library

The Tennessee River and its tributaries stretch across seven states in the central United States. This largely rural and undeveloped area was hard hit by the Depression. People who lived here were poor at the best of times. In 1933, it was a daily struggle just to stay alive. To add to their misery, brutal annual floods ruined their crops and swept away their housing. This is an example of flood damage in that area.

To alleviate this misery and to develop the economy of the region, the New Deal created the Tennessee Valley Authority (TVA), the largest reclamation and power project ever undertaken. A series of dams were built to control the river and forever end the floods. The TVA opened the river to barge traffic so that farmers were able to get their produce to market. Power generated by these dams provided cheap energy so that towns and farms could have the benefits of electricity. TVA is now the nation's largest producer of electricity. Millions of acres of reclaimed land were put into production with the help of new fertilizers, hybrid crops, and conservation techniques. These efforts produced new jobs, new industry, and new wealth. This dam is named after Senator George Norris, an early sponsor of the TVA.

Franklin D. Rossevelt Presidential Library

Franklin D. Roosevelt Presidential Library

Roosevelt's knowledge of rural Georgia and his many inspection trips through the Dust Bowl states gave him first-hand knowledge of the desperate condition of American farmers. In this photo, he talks with Steve Brown, a farmer in Jamestown, North Dakota. Many of the New Deal programs providing load guarantees, crop subsidies, and land conservation helped family farms weather the years of drought.

Franklin D. Rossevelt Presidential Library

Times were hard in the cities too. This photo shows a breadline in Manhattan. Out-of-work white-collar men line up in their suits and ties, fedoras and polished shoes; blue-collar workers line up wearing caps and jackets. All wait for a handout to keep their families and themselves from starving.

National Parks and History Association

Breadlines were a common sight in cities and towns across America. This is poignantly depicted in George Segal's sculpture at the Franklin Delano Roosevelt Memorial in Washington, D. C.

Franklin D. Rosevelt Presidential Library

People who had been fired from their jobs and evicted from their homes were forced to live in shacks like those shown in photo. This family had been "squatters" here for three years. Such shanty towns were called "Hoovervilles" in ironic tribute to former President Hoover who had done little to relieve hunger and want.

Franklin D. Rosevelt Presidential Library

Businesses failed, stores stood vacant, there was no work. Even though this cafe charged only 5¢ for "mush and milk," it went broke. Even though this building was listed with three realty companies, there were no takers. An out-of-work man leans against the building, slumped in despair. In a few short weeks, the New Deal put millions of men like this back to work, earning a paycheck, able to feed their families, and pay the rent.

The Works Project Administration (WPA) put millions of men to work across the nation, building schools, roads, parks, and utilities. Critics said that WPA workers were loafers "leaning on their shovels," but this was not true. Much good work was accomplished and men regained the dignity of being able to provide food and shelter for their families. These men are pushing wheelbarrows on a road project.

Franklin D. Rossevelt Presidential Library

Franklin D. Rossevelt Presidential Library

The Civilian Conservation Corps (CCC), run by the Army, took more than 5 million unemployed young men to work in the countryside. "CCC boys" built roads and tourist facilities in national parks and forests. They worked on reforestation and land conservation projects. For the first time in their lives, many had healthy diets and regular health care; many were taught to read and write; and many learned a trade. When war came, the fit, disciplined CCC boys became a core for the greatly enlarged U. S. military.

Franklin D. Rossevelt Presidential Library

Thanks to Eleanor Roosevelt and her allies, the New Deal programs were extended to women and minorities. This is a Tupelo, Mississippi, class of girls learning to be library workers.

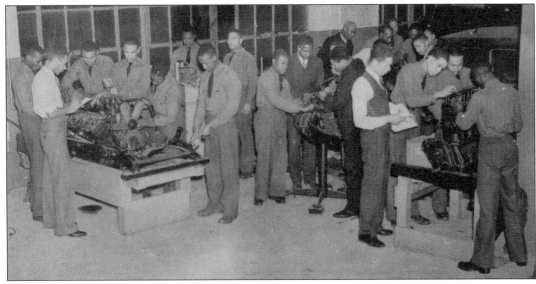

Franklin D. Rossevelt Presidential Library

In spite of the objections of conservative southern members of Congress, Blacks as well as whites participated in CCC programs. This class in auto mechanics took place in Richmond, Virginia.

The times were grim. President Roosevelt's challenge was great but he met it with leadership, confidence, and good cheer. FDR was truly the "Happy Warrior." In this photo, he throws out the first ball of the 1935 baseball season, a game between the Washington Senators and the New York Yankees.

Franklin D. Rossevelt Presidential Library

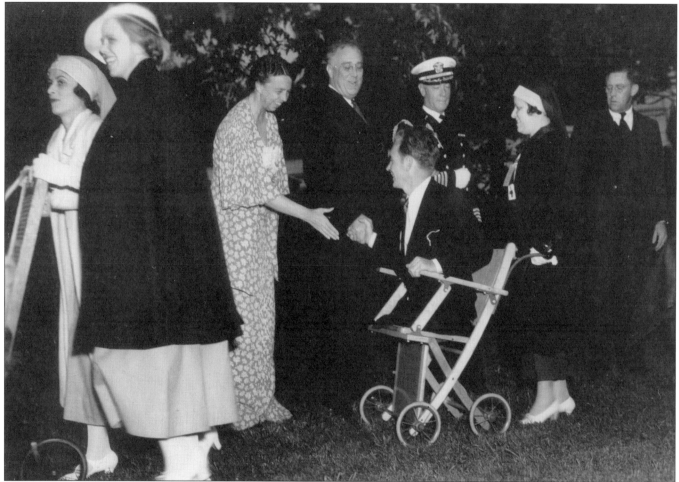

Franklin D. Roosevelt Presidential Library

Over the years, many thousands of Americans were invited to the White House to share in the Roosevelts' hospitality. At this garden party, the president and first lady greet veterans wounded in World War I. U. S. Navy Captain Brown, at FDR's side, provides a strong arm, which the President uses to stabilize his balance so as not to fall.

Franklin D. Roosevelt Presidential Library

Chapter *8*

"That Man in the White House"

The president was always a Navy man. He loved the sea. He read naval history as a hobby, collected ship models and had a real understanding of naval operations. He was assistant secretary of the Navy during World War I. In this photo, the Commander-in-Chief, surrounded by his admirals in dress uniform, reviews the fleet in New York harbor. He is aboard the cruiser, USS Indianapolis.

Roosevelt ran for reelection in 1936. Critics from the left and the right filled the airwaves and editorial pages with shrill and, sometimes scurrilous, denunciations of "That Man In The White House." Huey Long had been shot and killed in Louisiana in 1935, but a rabble-rouser named Gerald L. K. Smith leapt to take his place. Smith, Coughlin, the Liberty League, Wall Street bankers, and industrialists were at FDR's throat. These people hated President and Mrs. Roosevelt. FDR concluded to an advisor, "There is only one issue in this campaign. It's myself and people must be either for me or against me."

The Republicans nominated a nice, if colorless, man named Alf Landon to run against FDR. Landon was governor of Kansas, a Teddy Roosevelt Republican, who in spite of the Depression and the devastation of the dust bowl had managed to keep his state budget balanced. Landon was unknown outside Kansas.

The Democrats renominated the president in June. In his acceptance speech, speaking before 100,000 people, Roosevelt accepted the challenge. He struck out at the powerful business and banking interests that had tried to block his New Deal programs at every turn: "These economic royalists complain that we seek to overturn the institutions of America. What they really complain of is that we seek to take away their power."

As the election campaign began, the president remained above the fray. In the fall of 1935 he took a "nonpolitical" 3000-mile swing around the country. Inspecting New Deal programs, he also met with politicians and reporters at every stop and spoke often to crowds from the back platform of his train.

In the summer of 1936, Roosevelt toured Texas and the Midwest. It was another "nonpolitical" trip, said the White House. FDR's stated purpose was to visit historic sites and national parks, yet he found time to meet politicians and the press and to speak to the crowds gathered along his route.

His formal campaign did not begin until the end of September. The opposition had been bitter and better financed than FDR's side. He made campaign speeches in the major cities. In the last speech of the campaign in New York's Madison Square Garden, he lashed out against his enemies and railed against the powerful and united forces of industrial capitalism:

"Never before in all our history have these forces been so united against one candidate as they stand today. They are unanimous in their hatred for me—and I welcome their hatred! I should like it said of my first administration that in it the forces of selfishness and of lust for power met their match. I should like to have it said of my second administration that in it these

forces met their masters."

On election day, FDR won by a landslide with the largest majority in history. He carried every state but Maine and Vermont. Roosevelt was at the height of his power and popularity: a poll of Americans showed that eight out of every ten Americans liked him as a person. In his speech on Inauguration Day, he said, "I see one third of the nation ill housed, ill clad, ill nourished." He would use his great mandate from the people to advance the New Deal's philosophy. He said, "The test of our progress is not whether we add more to the abundance of those who have too much; it is whether we provide enough for those who have too little."

The election victory had been sweet, but soon enough things began to go sour. The United States Supreme Court, or the "Nine Old Men," as the young New Dealers called the justices, were conservatives appointed by the conservative Republican presidents Harding, Coolidge, and Hoover. The Court looked with horror on the New Deal programs and the growth of the federal government necessary to administer them. Starting in 1935, the Court, defining the federal authority to regulate interstate commerce in the narrowest possible terms, declared first one and then another of the New Deal laws to be unconstitutional and therefore void. These were laws the president had asked for, the Congress had approved and the public had supported with their votes.

In public FDR kept his cool, but underneath, he was furious. He would not let the Supreme Court dismantle the New Deal. Working in private with his attorney general, telling no one of his plans, Roosevelt drew up a proposal that would, in effect, alter the checks and balances by which our Federal system operates.

Without warning or consultation, President Roosevelt sent a message to Congress seeking authority to "pack" the Supreme Court. For every justice who failed to retire at the age of seventy, FDR would be able to add a new justice to the bench, up to a maximum of 15. This simple request stunned the country. It not only appalled conservatives; many liberals opposed this tampering with the balance of power among the three great branches of government: the executive, the legislative and the judicial.

FDR sent his message on February 5, and Congress exploded. Vice President "Cactus Jack" Garner, the Senate and House leadership, and the Democratic committee chairmen in Congress—all were in opposition. The debates on the proposal went on for months. There were angry speeches, parliamentary maneuvers, and a filibuster. The vice president went home to Texas rather than support the bill to pack the Supreme Court. Chief Justice Charles Evans Hughes violated all precedent and actively lobbied against it. On July 14, after many, many hours of acrimonious debate, the Senate Majority Leader, Joseph Robinson (D, Arkansas), dropped dead of a heart attack on the Senate floor, clutching a transcript of the debate in his hand. A week later, FDR was forced to concede defeat. Roosevelt had suffered a humiliating blow. Worse was to come.

Throughout 1936, the economy continued its recovery, employment increased and the stock market regained much of its vigor. New Deal pump-priming programs were working. And then, on Black Tuesday in October of 1937, the stock market collapsed. By the end of the year, two million workers had lost their jobs and steel production was off by three-fourths. Things began to look as bad as 1933. Roosevelt was stunned. His advisors say he was puzzled, discouraged and frustrated. Economists were divided, as economists always are, as to what should be done. It was open season on FDR; he took criticism from all across the political spectrum. It was called the Roosevelt Recession. At the end of 1937, FDR asked the Congress for even more emergency funds, sending the budget further into deficit. "I am going to go ahead and take care of the unemployed no matter how much it costs," he said. His stock on Capitol Hill had sunk so low that it was six months before Congress approved the money to put the unemployed back to work.

As if these setbacks were not enough, Roosevelt suffered another severe rebuke from the Congress in April 1938. He had asked the Congress to approve a reorganization of the executive branch, that had been worked out by an impartial committee of experts. It was designed to improve the efficiency of the White House and the executive agencies. Congressional conservatives, many of them southern Democrats, were outraged. This would give the president "the powers of a dictator!" a senator shouted. Many people agreed. It can happen here, they said, pointing to Europe where democracies were falling to Fascist dictators in Italy, Germany, Hungary, Spain. Commentators and editorials took up the cry of "dictator." So great became the din that FDR felt forced to issue an extraordinary statement:

1. I have no inclination to become a dictator.
2. I have none of the qualifications which would make me a successful dictator.
3. I have too much historical background and too much knowledge of existing dictatorships to make me desire any form of dictatorship for a democracy like the United States of America.

Denials had no impact on the Congress. In April 1938, the reorganization plan was killed in the House, amidst wild cheering and angry shouts. The Congress was in open revolt.

FDR got mad. The ranking congressional members of his own party, the powerful committee chairmen who controlled legislation, had turned against him and the New Deal. In his anger, he made what was the worst political mistake of his life. He would "purge" the Democratic party of those "obstructionist" members who opposed him and his policies. He would take sides in those state primaries where a liberal Democrat was trying to topple an incumbent conservative Democrat. Roosevelt went across the country, interfering with local politics. He spoke out against such men as Senators Walter George of Georgia, "Cotton" Ed Smith of South Carolina, Millard Tydings of Maryland, Guy Gillette of Iowa. This was a high-stakes game, risky in the extreme.

Roosevelt lost. Across the board, the old and powerful senators, now irrevocably against him, were reelected. The voters resented a president telling them how to vote in their local elections. Not long after FDR's repudiation, Senator George met Senator Smith on the floor of the Senate. George remarked, "You know, Roosevelt is his own worst enemy." "Not so long as I am alive!" replied Smith.

Franklin D. Rossevelt Presidential Library

During his presidency, Roosevelt tried to be at Warm Springs every year for Thanksgiving dinner with the polio patients. The president would broadcast Thanksgiving greetings to the nation from there. The President and Mrs. Roosevelt would sit at head table with the patients and carve the turkey. At the end of the evening, the president would sit at the door and shake hands and chat with each of the patients.

When he was staying at the Little White House, the president would drive his hand-controlled car down to the front gate of the rehab center's grounds for an impromptu press conference with White House reporters. The president met with the press at the White House at least twice a week; at Warm Springs it was almost daily.

Franklin D. Rossevelt Presidential Library

Franklin D. Roosevelt Presidential Library

Franklin D. Roosevelt Presidential Library

President Roosevelt made many cross-country inspection tours. He rode in the railroad car, the Ferdinand Magellan, *specially built for his use by the Pullman Company. At each stop, FDR would address the large and enthusiastic crowds gathered to see him. The White House denied these trips were in any way political but, over the course of his 12 years in office, millions of Americans got to see their president in person. Here the president speaks in Booneville, Arkansas. On the platform with him is Senator Hattie Carroway, the first woman ever to be elected to the U. S. Senate.*

Roosevelt just loved watching the scenery in his swings across the country. His train moved at a slow 35 miles an hour so that he could see the countryside and, incidentally, be seen by the people lining the track. In this 1938 photo, his train has stopped at the bottom of the Royal Gorge on the Denver & Rio Grande Western line, west of Canon City, Colorado. FDR knew a good photo opportunity when he saw one.

FDR was a skillful politician and he loved the gatherings of the Democratic party faithful. In this photo, he is seated in a large chair at the center of the head table at the 1939 Jackson Day dinner held in the ballroom of the Mayflower Hotel, Washington, D.C. With a glass of wine in one hand and his famous cigarette holder in the other, the president is having a fine time.

Franklin D. Rossevelt Presidential Library

Bettman/Corbis

At the same 1939 Jackson Day dinner, Roosevelt is seen with John Nance Garner of Texas. Garner, a Texan, was FDR's Vice President during his first two terms. Garner is remembered for saying the Vice Presidency is "not worth a warm bucket of spit." People differ over whether "spit" is the exact word the VP used.

Franklin D. Roosevelt Presidential Library

Franklin D. Roosevelt Presidential Library

In the 1936 election, as in 1932, FDR waged a masterful campaign. Huge crowds turned out to hear him speak. At left, he gives a campaign speech in Topeka, Kansas. Center, he meets a little girl, Helen Virginia Sewell, in Atlanta, Georgia. Roosevelt campaigned rain or shine. At right, wet and smiling, FDR greets the crowd on a rainy day.

Franklin D. Roosevelt Presidential Library

During FDR's second term, the New Deal construction projects were on the way to completion. This photo shows the north half of the great Bonneville Dam across the Columbia River, 40 miles east of Portland, Oregon. This Public Works Administration dam provides power to the entire Northwest and has made Portland an oceangoing port.

Franklin D. Rossevelt Presidential Library

Franklin D. Roosevelt Presidential Library

This photo shows Oregon's Timberline Lodge, built high on the slopes of Mt. Hood. Under the auspices of the New Deal, the lodge was built by out-of-work craftsmen and women. Only local stone and timber were used. All hinges, handles, and hardware were hand-forged. All furniture was handmade; curtains and linens were woven by hand. Roosevelt dedicated both the Timberline Lodge and nearby Bonneville Dam during his 1937 western tour.

Franklin D. Roosevelt Presidential Library

On a tour of the segregated South in 1939, Roosevelt met famed African American agronomist, George Washington Carver, at Tuskegee Institute, Tuskegee, Alabama. At Roosevelt's insistence, a polio rehabilitation center, similar to the one at Warm Springs, was built here for the treatment of black patients.

Franklin D. Rossevelt Presidential Library

The New Deal provided work for out-of-work artists. This wall mural was commissioned for the Central Post Office, New York City. Painted by Louis Lozowick, it depicts a steam-powered towboat pushing a barge backed by the Manhattan skyline.

Franklin D. Rossevelt Presidential Library

The WPA Federal Theater Project gave work to actors and stage technicians in cities and towns across the country. This photo shows the Jewish Theater Unit of New York City presenting an evening of comedy and klezmer band music.

Franklin D. Rossevelt Presidential Library

In June 1939, the King and Queen of England made a state visit to the United States for the first time. After the formal ceremonies in Washington, D. C., the Roosevelts hosted the royal couple for a weekend at Hyde Park. At a picnic, Mrs. Roosevelt invited the neighbors and served the King and Queen the usual picnic fare — hot dogs and potato salad. The visit built much American goodwill for Britain, which proved its value when Britain went to war with Nazi Germany, three months later.

Washington Post Co., Martin Luther King Public Library, Washington, D.C.

Chapter *9*

Roosevelt vs Hitler

Franklin and Eleanor Roosevelt return to the White House after his third inauguration as president of the United States, January 20, 1941. Roosevelt felt obliged to run for a third term as war loomed in both the Pacific and Atlantic. The "isolationist" opposition refused to support assistance to the democracies at war or rearmament at home and they voted against the draft.

Aerica had fought World War I with gusto, but the peace had gone sour. Europe returned to its usual European squabbles of border clashes, secret treaties, revolutions, and ethnic wars. America wanted none of it. The United States would take care of itself and to hell with the rest of the world. America First!

But the United States is a trading nation. In 1940 its economy depended on trade with Europe and the Far East. Great ocean liners crossed the Atlantic in four days. Passenger air service now crisscrossed the continent. You could even fly to Europe with stops in the Azores and Lisbon or fly to Asia by way of Hawaii and Midway Island. Radio and telephone spanned the world. Newsreels and wire photos brought the world into every home. Americans were not as remote or protected as they thought they were.

In 1933, Adolph Hitler rose to power as the Nazi fuhrer of Germany. Benito Mussolini was the Fascist dictator of Italy. In the Soviet Union, dictator Joseph Stalin ruled with an iron hand, slaughtering millions of his citizens in the process. Spain was wracked by civil war between the elected Republican government and the Fascist supporters of Generalissimo Francisco Franco. With the help of Germany and Italy, Franco smashed the

Republicans. France was governed, if that is the word for it, by a series of incompetent, arrogant and corrupt men. It built the Maginot Line, a wall the length of its border with Germany, with the naive belief that a wall could protect it from attack. Britain was wallowing in high unemployment and labor unrest. Its leaders felt that pacifism was a good thing and that appeasement—giving the dictators what they wanted—would keep the peace.

In the Far East, Japanese policy was controlled by the military. Under the umbrella of forming a Greater East Asia Co-Prosperity Sphere, Japan was determined to subjugate all of Asia. In 1931, the Japanese marched into Manchuria, changed its name to Manchuko, and set up a puppet government. In 1932, the Japanese invaded Shanghai. In 1937, Japan launched a full-scale invasion of China. Fighting was fierce and inconclusive.

After the capture of the Chinese city of Nanking, December 13, 1937, Japanese troops raped, maimed and killed more than 300,000 of its citizens. In the Spanish Civil War, the German *Luftwaffe,* anxious to try out its new warplanes, destroyed the village of Guernica, bombing its buildings, strafing its people. Newsreels and still photos showed America the new horrors of a modern warfare in which noncombatant citizens—old men, women, and children—became just another target.

Inside Germany, the Nazis killed, tortured, and interned those it considered enemies of the state and those it considered subhuman—first the mentally and physically disabled, then the Jews, Gypsies, people of color, gays, criminals, alcoholics, and so on. Breaking treaties and agreements, Hitler began a massive German rearmament. Japan and Italy were also arming at a alarming rate.

In 1936, Hitler marched into the Rhineland and no one stopped him. In 1937, he signed anti-Communist treaties of alliance with Italy and Japan, thus forming the Axis powers. In 1938, he annexed Austria, and rode triumphant through Vienna to the delirious cheers of more than a million Austrians. And no one stopped him.

In the spring of 1939, Czechoslovakia had an army of a million men, well armed by the state-of-the-art Skoda arms works. Using infiltration, bribes and threats, and in spite of the futile pleas of Britain and France, who were bound by treaty to defend the country, Hitler seized Czechoslovakia without firing a shot.

Poland was now surrounded on three sides by Germany, and on the fourth by Communist Russia. Poland was a democracy; it was allied with the other democracies, Britain and France. Throughout the summer, Hitler made impossible demands of Poland that Poland refused to meet. Tensions were very high and went higher in August when Hitler signed a mutual nonaggression pact with Russia. Now Hitler, who despised Asians as an inferior race and called communism his greatest enemy, was allied with Russia and Japan. The Russo-German treaty stunned the world. Britain and France threatened to retaliate against Germany if Hitler moved on Poland. Hitler thought they were bluffing.

On September 1, 1939, Hitler called their bluff. He declared war on Poland. On September 3, Britain and France declared war on Germany. World War II had begun. The German Blitzkrieg, a combined assault of panzer divisions (tanks and armored vehicles) and air attack by Stuka dive-bombers and Messerschmitt fighters, wiped out Polish resistance in two weeks. Russia and Germany divided up Poland and Poland was no more.

All of this was in 1939. Americans saw it all in newsreels at the movies, in *Life* magazine and, on their radios, they heard live overseas reports from Berlin, Paris, and London. Americans could hear Hitler's speeches, hysterical tirades of shouting and hate, and the response of the German people, "*Sieg Heil! Sieg Heil! Sieg Heil!,*" long into the night.

Roosevelt had warned the American people of danger. In 1937, in his famous quarantine speech, he said, "The peace-loving nations must make a concerted effort in opposition to those [who] are creating a state of international anarchy and instability from which there is no escape through mere isolation or neutrality. When an epidemic of physical disease starts to spread, the community . . . joins in a quarantine to protect the health of the community." Was he calling for international cooperation to isolate the aggressive nations? FDR did not say; he was in a bind. He could not lead unless the nation was prepared to follow, and it was not. Americans didn't like such talk. A poll of voters showed that 19 out of 20 answered "no" to the question "Should the United States participate in another world war?" The isolationists in the Congress would have none of it, either. The 1938 congressional elections were a repudiation of Roosevelt's policies, both at home and abroad. The isolationist Republicans doubled their representation in the House. They would not allow America to rearm; they would not allow a call-up of young men to the armed forces. They would not allow the sale of airplanes or tanks or ships to help the democracies defend themselves. It is Europe's business, and none of our own, they said.

When war in Europe began, FDR tried to bring the com-batants to the peace table. His efforts were rebuffed by the democracies and ridiculed by the dictators. Hitler laughed at Roosevelt, thought he was crazy. Hitler said FDR's paralysis was caused by late-stage syphilis that had now probably advanced to his brain.

Roosevelt warned the nation again: "When peace has been broken anywhere, the peace of all countries everywhere is endangered." The American Neutrality Act prevented selling arms and munitions to either side in the European war. Roosevelt asked Congress to repeal the act, reasoning that if the democracies were to make their stand against Nazi tyranny, they needed American help. But this was the Congress that had blocked him on Supreme Court appointments; it was led by men he had tried to purge. FDR pulled out all the stops for repeal—bribing congressmen with patronage and appropriations, pleading with Republican leaders through third parties, and urging publishers and industrialists to support him on repeal. He was supported by The Non-Partisan Committee for Revision of the Neutrality Law, directed by the much loved and widely respected Republican, William Allen White. In violent opposition were the America First organization, led by the genuine all-American hero, Charles Lindbergh; the old Liberty Lobby; Father Coughlin and his rabble-rousers; and even the German-American Bund. Debate roared in the Congress. It was only after the fall of Poland that repeal was passed in favor of a "cash-and-carry" policy. This policy meant that either side could buy all the arms they wanted, as long as they paid up front in cash and carried them away in their own ships. This sounded neutral, but in fact, it favored the democratic Allies, as the British Royal Navy had set up an effective blockade of Germany.

The 1930s had been ". . . a low and dishonest decade," said poet W. H. Auden. If 1939 was bad; 1940 would be worse, much worse. In March, 1940, Russia invaded Finland. Italy, having conquered Ethiopia, seized Albania. On April 9, Denmark fell to German troops; it took little more than an hour. Norway was invaded; it fell in several days. On May 10, Hitler turned his terrifying Blitzkrieg on western Europe: parachute troops, screaming dive bombers, panzer divisions, and behind them, came 120 crack infantry divisions and 6,000 warplanes. Holland and Belgium fell in an instant. The Nazis trapped the British and French forces in a pincer movement by passing through the "impassible" Ardennes forest. By June 4, the British Expeditionary Forces had been driven to the sea at Dunkirk. They were rescued only by a miracle of weather, calm seas, and thousands of English pleasure boats, tugboats, and anything else able to cross the English Channel. By June 11, it was all over. Hitler, riding down the Champs-Elysees of Paris in his open staff car, occupied the north of France and set up a puppet government in the south. Hitler had achieved in one month what, in World War I, the Germans had failed to achieve in five years of fighting. He now controlled the land mass of Europe, and Britain stood alone. The victorious Hitler ordered that planning begin for the invasion of Britain.

Thus began the Battle of Britain. In Parliament the appeaser, Prime Minister Neville Chamberlain, resigned, and the "old lion," Winston S. Churchill, took the helm of a national coalition government. At that critical moment, his valiant speeches were more powerful than weapons. He rallied the British people with words that echo down the years. He said:

We shall defend our island, whatever the cost may be, we shall fight on the beaches, we shall fight on the landing grounds, we shall fight in the fields and in the streets, we shall fight in the hills, we shall never surrender.

He warned, should Hitler triumph, "then the whole world including the United States, including all that we have known and cared for, will sink into the abyss of a new Dark Age. . . Let us therefore brace ourselves to our duties, and so bear ourselves that, if the British empire and commonwealth last for a thousand years, men will say, 'This was their finest hour.'"

In Washington, the New Deal was stymied, the Congress was angry. Roosevelt was tired, his polio-weakened muscles ached. He planned to retire at the end of his second term in 1940. Looking forward to this, he had designed and built a small cottage high on a hill in the woods of his Hyde Park estate. A library had also been built on the estate to house FDR's presidential papers. He planned to study and write history, sitting by the fire in his stone cottage in the woods.

The nation was in an uproar. The Republicans in Congress, almost to a man, were isolationist, resolutely opposed to American intervention in Europe. Many Americans felt the same way. Many, many other Americans saw the Nazi threat to this country. Already Nazi spies and collaborators were reported at work throughout South America. If the United States did nothing, did not rearm, did not send all possible aid to Britain, it would soon be the only democracy left. Democracy could not live in a Fascist world.

In the spring of 1940, it seemed the Republican candidate for president would be an isolationist. The available Democratic candidates were a sorry lot. Each had his supporters but no one candidate could rally support from across the broad spectrum of the Roosevelt coalition. No president had ever served a third term. Would Roosevelt run again? For many months, he would not say. He was busy. The White House and the agencies FDR created by executive order had become the clearinghouse for the rearming of America and the shipment of arms and materiel to Britain. The Great Depression was truly over as the vast might of American industry converted to wartime production. Britain desperately needed bombers. FDR saw that she got them, even over the protests of the chiefs of staff who said they were needed at home. Britain needed destroyers to protect against invasion and to hunt down German U-boats, submarines which were sinking British merchant marine ships at the rate of 50,00 tons every couple of days. Six hundred and twenty-two merchant ships were lost in the last six months of 1940. At great political danger to himself and acting probably illegally, FDR found a way to "swap" 50 old American Navy destroyers in exchange for the use of some British islands in the Caribbean. "Give us the tools and we will finish the job," Churchill told America. America would become the "arsenal of democracy," Roosevelt proclaimed.

The world was in flames. Millions of refugees clogged the roads of Europe. Vast atrocities were being committed: citizens were bombed and strafed, passenger ships were torpedoed. Extermination of the Jews was underway. Rotterdam was flattened, Warsaw destroyed. In the blitz, the bombing of London, Hitler sent more than a thousand planes a day over the city. The Commons, the lower house of Parliament, was destroyed; Buckingham Palace was damaged; the Cathedral of St. Paul's was lit by flames as the buildings surrounding it burned. More that 70,000 British citizens were killed by the blitz.

American opinion turned. Support for Britain grew as Nazi horrors mounted. Newsreels brought these atrocities to every movie theater. CBS correspondent, Edward R. Murrow broadcast nightly from England with "This is London Calling." Listeners could hear the bombs explode and the wail of the air raid sirens as Murrow reported on the blitz. William L. Shirer from Berlin and other correspondents broadcasting from across Europe brought the war to every American living room. Winston Churchill's great speeches were broadcast live in the United States.

Roosevelt was renominated by acclamation at the Democratic convention. His Republican opponent was Wendell Willkie. Willkie was a moderate Republican. He supported the New Deal programs, more or less, and aid to the Allies in their struggle against the Fascist dictators. In the campaign, however, the isolationists, the Ku Klux Klan, the crypto-Nazis, Communists, populists, industrialists and a whole variety of ists and isms who were supporting Willkie, forced him to make ever more extreme statements. Vote for Roosevelt and you vote for war he said. In response, the Democrats said, "Vote for Willkie, and you vote for Hitler." In the last weeks of the presidential campaign, Japan occupied all of Cambodia, Laos, and Vietnam. Italy invaded Greece. U. S. intelligence reported that Japan was mobilizing to take all of southeast Asia. German divisions were readying a 3-million-man invasion of Russia. It was thought the election would be close; the campaign was hard fought. On election day, however, the American people came down on the side of FDR. He won the election, 449 electoral votes to Willkie's 82.

Still Pictures Branch, National Archives and Records

All Europe was at war and Hitler was winning. By the end of 1940, the Nazi Blitzkrieg had defeated Poland, Holland, Belgium, Denmark, Norway, and France. Britain stood alone. Hitler launched the Battle of Britain: an intense blitz, night and day, of air raids over London and the English Channel port cities. Bomb damage was devastating. In this photo, Londoners go about their daily business, even as fire and rescue efforts continue from last night's air raids.

In London, thousands of buildings were destroyed and more than 50,000 lost their lives. For many months, people used the Underground subway stations as makeshift air raid shelters, spending their nights sleeping on the hard platforms. Hitler's blitz did not break the spirit of the Londoners.

May 10, 1940, the day Hitler's armies swept into Holland, Belgium and Luxemburg, Winston Churchill became Prime Minister of Great Britain. His courageous leadership saved Britain from defeat in the 17 months before America entered the war. Roosevelt and Churchill worked closely together throughout World War II in what was called the "Grand Alliance."

The leaders of Nazi Germany were riding high. They were determined that Germany would rule supreme over all the world, "Deutschland Uber Alles." Here they are, the Nazi Leadership Corps: (left to right) Reichfuhrer S. S. Heinrich Himmler (behind Hitler), Fuhrer Adolf Hitler, Reich Marshall Hermann Goering, propaganda chief Goebbels, and Rudolf Hess.

By 1940, Japan controlled Indochina and half of China; and it intended to conquer all of South East Asia. Atrocities committed by Japanese soldiers were documented in American newsreels and newsmagazines. This picture was taken during the "Rape of Nanking," in which rampaging Japanese soldiers murdered some 300,000 civilians and raped an estimated 10,000 women. Here Japanese soldiers bayonet defenseless civilians.

In 1940, over the strong objections of Congressional "isolationists," Congress narrowly approved the Selective Service Act, the first peacetime military conscription in American history. All young men were required to register for the draft; a million men were called up into military service. Here, under the eyes of President Roosevelt, Secretary of War Henry Stimson draws the numbers of the first men to be drafted. The ceremony was broadcast nationwide by radio.

In the face of danger, Roosevelt declared that America must become "the arsenal of democracy." The United States began producing aircraft, ships, and tanks on an ever-increasing scale. America rearmed and supplied all the war materiel it could to Britain, albeit on a "cash-and-carry" basis. These fighter airplanes are loaded and on their way to England.

Franklin D. Rossevelt Presidential Library

Franklin D. Rossevelt Presidential Library

FDR had planned to retire at the end of his second term in 1940. With this in mind, he built a small stone cottage on his estate in Hyde Park. Reached only by a rough dirt road, Top Cottage became his hideaway. Here he planned to live with his books and papers. In this informal setting, he entertained Winston Churchill, King George VI, Queen Elizabeth of Great Britain and other VIPs. In these photos Eleanor and Franklin Roosevelt are shown in the living room of Top Cottage.

In 1940, FDR acquired a Scottie named Fala. Wherever the President went, Fala went with him. Fala quickly became the most famous dog in America. MGM even made a documentary about his life in the White House, with the President playing a supporting role. Here is Fala with his master on the back platform of Roosevelt's train.

In this photo, Fala hurries to get into FDR's car.

Franklin D. Rossevelt Presidential Library

Franklin D. Rossevelt Presidential Library

Still Pictures Branch, National Archives and Records

Chapter *10*

Commander in Chief

FDR knew that the destroyer swap with Britain would raise hell with the Republicans and the Congress. Even though it was done in the middle of his reelection campaign, Roosevelt completed the deal. The destroyers were needed by the British, so he did it. During that fall of 1940, FDR pushed through passage of the Selective Service Act, which allowed the government to draft men into the army. It was the first peacetime conscription in American history and very controversial. Senator Burton K. Wheeler of Montana warned that "the draft would lead to dictatorship." "Mr. Roosevelt today committed an act of war," said the *St. Louis Post Dispatch*. He also became "America's first dictator." The draft was so unpopular that a year later the Congress, just three months before the Japanese attack on Pearl Harbor, came within one vote of ending it and disbanding the enlarged army.

British shipping continued to suffer huge losses from Nazi U-boats. In the name of American security and to help the British, Roosevelt declared a "security zone" extending halfway across the Atlantic to be patrolled by the U. S. Navy. He seized Danish Greenland to keep it from falling into Nazi hands. He

PEARL HARBOR! On December 7, 1941, "a date that will live in infamy," forces of the Japanese Empire attacked the home port of the U. S. Pacific Fleet at Pearl Harbor on the island of Oahu, Hawaii. It was a Sunday morning and the attack was a complete surprise. Damage to American forces was devastating.

extended American protection over Iceland. He secretly authorized the U. S. Navy to report the location of U-boat "wolf packs" to the Royal Navy. Soon American destroyers began "patrolling" convoys bound for Britain. FDR called it "patrolling" because escorting belligerent ships would constitute an act of war. In fact, merchant shipping convoys were escorted safely through the security zone by the U. S. Navy, at which point they would be handed over to the Royal Navy and escorted into British ports..

Fully as serious as losses at sea was the fact that Britain was running out of money. It no longer had the "cash" to "carry" the arms, munitions and food it needed to survive. A month after the election, Roosevelt explained to the American people why it was important to keep supplying Britain. "The best immediate defense of the United States is to help Britain defend itself . . . it is . . . important from a selfish point of view that we should do everything to help." To this end, FDR proposed the Lend-Lease Act. America would "lend' Britain the arms it needed and not worry about "the dollar . . . that silly old dollar sign." After all, he explained, "If my neighbor's house catches fire, I lend him my garden hose and let him use my hydrant. I don't say to him, now neighbor . . . you've got to pay me $15 [the cost of the hose]." The debate over this act in the Congress was brutal. Lend-Lease policy "will plough under every fourth American boy," a senator shouted. After two months of heated debate, Lend-Lease was approved by the Congress. "It was," Churchill told the Parliament, "the most unsordid act in the history of any nation."

In his State of the Union message to the Congress, January 6, 1941, Roosevelt first enunciated what became the war aims of the nations allied in the war against Hitler, the Four Freedoms:

> In the future days, which we seek to make secure, we look forward to a world founded upon four essential human freedoms. The first is freedom of speech and expression—everywhere in the world. The second is freedom of every person to worship God in his own way—everywhere in the world. The third is freedom from want—everywhere in the world. The fourth is freedom from fear—anywhere in the world.

America's support of Britain enraged Hitler. The fuhrer absolutely despised Roosevelt; thought he was crazy. Not only that, he was sure FDR was part Jewish because he "acted like a tortuous pettifogging Jew" and "the completely Negroid features of his wife showed that she too was a half-cast." Hitler confided to his aides that, although America was a great power with great resources, its government was incompetent and the United States could not prevent his defeat of Great Britain or the fulfillment of his plans for the Soviet Union.

In 1940, U. S. intelligence broke Japan's top-secret code. Now there was now no doubt that Japan was going to war in east Asia. American military knew Japan would strike but did not know where. Many thought it would be the Philippines, then a U. S. possession. Roosevelt tried to forestall Japan with endless negotiations, even appeasement. America was rearming, but it needed time. It was strengthening its fleet; building up its Pacific bases; training its new army of draftees; and supplying Britain, all at the same time. But time was short in the Pacific. In November 1940, Japanese Prime Minister Tojo told the world, "We must purge this [western presence] from east Asia with a vengeance."

On May 27, 1941, Roosevelt issued a proclamation of "extreme national emergency." America was now in a state of "limited war." On June 22, without warning, Germany attacked its erstwhile partner, Russia, with 130 divisions divided into three armies. The Nazi Blitzkrieg into Russia was terrible to behold. The Russians lost 2,000 planes in the first 24 hours. Western and German opinion believed that Russian resistance would collapse within a month or two. It did not. The Germans advanced far into Russia, but they had to fight every step of the way. Come winter, the German armies were deep into Russia, their supply lines stretched to the breaking point. German soldiers fought in the sub-zero Russian winter without overcoats—headquarters had not planned on a winter campaign. The Nazis could kill Russians by the hundreds of thousands, but still there were more, fighting for "Holy Mother Russia." It was the most bloody, brutal front in the war. By war's end, at least 6 million Russian soldiers and 2.6 million German soldiers had been killed. Roosevelt sent Lend-Lease aid to bolster Russian defenses. He and Churchill now agreed that Communist Russia must be kept fighting Hitler at whatever cost. As Churchill told the Parliament, "If Hitler invaded Hell, I should find occasion to make a favorable reference to the Devil."

The Axis powers, Germany, Japan and Italy, made two great mistakes in World War II:

• Hitler, in violation of his nonaggression pact, invaded

Russia before he had defeated Britain. His armies were trapped in Russia. With America's entry into the war, the invasion of Nazi-occupied western Europe became inevitable. Hitler's ability to fight in the West was hindered by his involvement in the east. Hitler now faced a two-front war.

• Japan brought America into the war with its surprise attack on Pearl Harbor in Hawaii on December 7, 1941, "a date that will live in infamy," as FDR called it. The United States declared war on Japan; then Germany declared war on the United States. America's vast resources, its huge industrial machine, its great pool of labor, if used wisely and to the full, made it a well nigh invincible foe.

Pearl Harbor was the major American naval base in the Pacific. The Japanese attack was devastating, disabling or destroying 8 battleships, 3 cruisers, 4 other vessels, 188 warplanes, and shore installations, and causing 3,435 casualties. The Japanese lost 28 warplanes. Over the next weeks, the Japanese swept over south Asia, conquering Hong Kong and most of China, Malaya, Burma, Singapore, the Dutch East Indies (now Indonesia), and the major island chains of the south Pacific.

No American alive at the time has forgotten Pearl Harbor Day. The shock of it was overwhelming; the extent of it was unbelievable. In the days after the Japanese attack, Roosevelt demonstrated anew his very skill as leader. On that Sunday, December 7, he met with his cabinet and then with the congressional leadership. He was grim yet confident. He was firm in direction and clear about what must be done. That night he dictated in full his message to Congress.

Roosevelt delivered this message the next day before a

joint session of Congress. With his chin out-thrust, his voice both calm and solemn, he called upon Congress for a declaration of war against the Empire of Japan. FDR expressed the determination of the entire nation when he assured the world, "The American people in their righteous might will win through to absolute victory." Under Secretary of State Sumner Welles later wrote that during this critical period Roosevelt "demonstrated the ultimate capacity to dominate and control a supreme emergency, which is the rarest and most valuable characteristic of any statesman."

Under FDR's leadership, interventionists and isolationists, Democrats and Republicans united in their determination to win the war. President Roosevelt brought distinguished Republicans into his Cabinet: Henry Stimson as secretary of war, Frank Knox as secretary of the navy. The heads of major companies came to Washington to administer the massive mobilization buildup. Many of them, the "dollar-a-year men," worked for nothing but a token $1 a year. Virtually without exception, these industrialists and Wall Street attorneys meshed well with FDR and came to respect and revere the man they had previously so reviled. One of them, John J. McCloy, was with Roosevelt once when he took a political phone call. Backing out of the room, McCloy demurred, "I am a Republican." "Oh, I keep forgetting that!" laughed the president.

Still Pictures Branch, National Archives and Records

Eight battleships were lined up along "Battleship Row." The Arizona *was sunk with more than 1,000 crew members trapped inside. The* Oklahoma *was also sunk. The* California *was disabled. The* Tennessee *capsized and the flooded* West Virginia *was lodged on a mud bank. The* Nevada *took direct hits, and was beached before she sunk. Over 150 planes were destroyed; a 100 more were damaged.*

Franklin D. Rossevelt Presidential Library

Franklin D. Rossevelt Presidential Library

If the Japanese could bomb Hawaii, anything was possible. Americans panicked. There were reports of Japanese submarines shelling the West Coast (true) and Japanese warplanes over San Diego and Los Angeles (false). In the ensuing hysteria, the federal government rounded up all persons of Japanese ancestry living on the West Coast and kept them interned in detention camps for the duration of the war. The headline on these newspaper tell the story.

Americans were furious. War was declared against Japan and Germany. Millions of American men and women enlisted in the military, singing, "Remember Pearl Harbor as We Go to Meet the Foe." The U. S. economy went into all-out war production. President Roosevelt and shipyard owner, Henry J. Kaiser, watch as the Victory Ship, SS Joseph N. Teal, slides down the ways in Portland, Oregon. The Teal was built in but ten days.

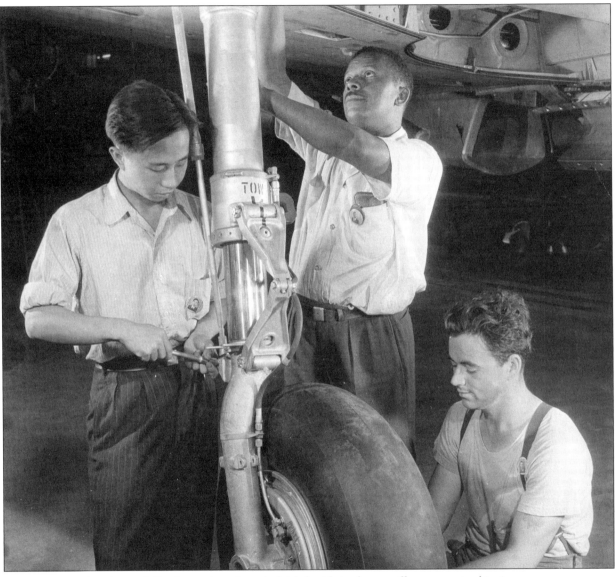

Franklin D. Roosevelt Presidential Library

Americans of all colors and creeds worked side by side in the war effort, as seen in this picture.
With the migration of large numbers of African Americans from the rural south to the northern
industrial cities to work in war plants, the cause of integration was advanced.

Franklin D. Roosevelt Presidential Library

"Rosie the Riveter" was more than just a popular song of the day. With so many men away at the war women took their places on the assembly line, marking a major step in the march toward women's equality. This photo shows three women mechanics at work on a fighter plane.

Franklin D. Roosevelt Presidential Library

Persons of short stature, "little people," often subject to social stigma, became valued workers in aircraft factories. They could work in tight spaces, inside wing and tail assemblies, where others could not fit.

Still Pictures Branch, National Archives and Records

Shipping war goods across the Atlantic was perilous business. Here members of the crew of the Victory Ship, SS Booker T. Washington, *relax in Cardiff, Wales, after a dangerous crossing of the sub-infested waters. The name of their puppy mascot is "Booker."*

Franklin D. Roosevelt Presidential Library

America became the "arsenal of democracy," as FDR called it. Through the Lend-Lease program, the United States was supplying Britain, Russia and China with massive amounts of war materiel. The photo shows row on row of field artillery pieces, newly arrived in England.

Still Pictures Branch, National Archives and Records

German U-boat submarines sank many U. S. and allied freighters in the North Atlantic. Most dangerous of all was the Murmansk Run. American ships, loaded with supplies for Russia, were forced to sail far north, above Scandinavia, across the Arctic Ocean to the port of Murmansk. The weather was horrible, the ocean ice cold, and U-boats always on the prowl. This photo was taken on the "Run."

Franklin D. Rossevelt Presidential Library

Boys and girls were let out from school to go door to door, collecting aluminum pots and pans, scrap metal, and newspapers, all for the war effort.

Housewives saved their grease and lard and their children carried it to collection points. The oils were used in making ammunition.

Franklin D. Rossevelt Presidential Library

Franklin D. Roosevelt Presidential Library

On the home front, food, clothing, gasoline, and tires were in short supply. To ensure fairness in distribution for all, a rationing system was set up. Americans of all ages, from school children to senior citizens, were urged to grow their own food, to plant "victory gardens" to supplement the food supply. In the cities, parks and vacant lots were plowed and subdivided into garden plots. Here the Secretary of Agriculture leads the way, plowing up Boston Commons.

Franklin D. Rossevelt Presidential Library

Even golf balls went to war! Here crooner, movie star, and well-known golfer, Bing Crosby, lends his presence to the campaign to collect old golf balls for the precious rubber they contain.

Franklin D. Roosevelt Presidential Library

Small towns, neighborhoods, even city blocks erected patriotic shrines with the names inscribed of their men serving in the military, those wounded, and those killed. This photo shows such a place, in a Chicago neighborhood. The local priest, American Legion members, and community leaders attend a war bond rally there.

Franklin D. Roosevelt Presidential Library

Shortly after Pearl Harbor, Japanese troops invaded the Philippines, then a colony of the United States. For four months, American and Philippine troops fought bravely, but they were overwhelmed. On May 6, 1942, the last American soldiers surrendered on the island of Corregidor where they had been living in caves to escape the intense Japanese bombardment. This Japanese photo shows their surrender.

Still Pictures Branch, National Archives and Records

The Japanese now controlled the entire Pacific and the outlook was bleak. However, in a daring move, General Jimmy Doolittle, commanding 16 B-25 twin bombers (as in this photo), bombed Tokyo on April 18, 1942. B-25s were land-based planes. Loaded with fuel, they barely made if off the flight deck of the carrier Hornet. *From Tokyo, they were forced to fly on and crash-land in China and Russia. The planes carried only four bombs each and they did little damage. However, the raid lifted American morale and served notice on Japan that its homeland was not safe.*

Still Pictures Branch, National Archives and Records

Chapter *11*

"Dr. Win the War"

Japanese aggression was stopped dead at the Battle of Midway, June 4, 1942. The Imperial Fleet was massive: 6 aircraft carriers, 11 battleships, 13 cruisers and 45 destroyers. The U. S. Fleet had but 3 aircraft carriers, 8 cruisers and 14 destroyers. In fierce air combat, the Americans managed to sink four Japanese carriers and damage the rest of the fleet. The Japanese fled in defeat. The Americans lost one carrier, the Yorktown. *She was sunk after receiving two direct torpedo hits. This Japanese torpedo bomber was destroyed as it attacked the ship.*

Winston Churchill arrived at the White House two weeks after Pearl Harbor. In this meeting and in others, Roosevelt and Churchill, with their military chiefs in tow, mapped a grand strategy to win the war: the principal effort would be to defeat Hitler. After that, the American and British navies would make short work of the Japanese. More than 3 million Nazi troops were engaged on the Russian front. Russia must be given all the supplies it needed to keep on fighting the Germans. From England, a combined British-American force would launch a massive invasion of Occupied France across the Channel. This effort would take a huge buildup of men and arms, and it would take time.

In the meantime, American forces would land in North Africa, take over Vichy French North Africa, and march to the assistance of British Field Marshall Bernard Montgomery, whose forces were being driven back into British-held Egypt by the crack Afrika Korps, commanded by the German "Desert Fox," General Erwin Rommel. Rommel had to be stopped so that the Suez Canal, between the Indian Ocean and the Mediterranean Sea, could be kept open to allow Middle East oil to fuel Britain and the Allied forces.

In those last dark days of December 1941, it warmed America, and indeed the world, to see the leaders of the United States and Great Britain standing together on the back porch of the White House to light the national Christmas tree. Addressing the nation, Roosevelt said, "Fellow workers for freedom . . . our strongest weapon in this war is that conviction of the dignity and brotherhood of man that Christmas represents . . ."

On New Year's Day, after frantic cabling among 26 countries, the two leaders issued a "Declaration of the United Nations." These 26 nations pledged to ". . . fight for complete victory [that] is essential to defend life, liberty, independence and religious freedom." This declaration was the genesis of today's United Nations.

Churchill and FDR had spent the previous evening searching for an appropriate name for the new organization. The next morning, Roosevelt threw open Churchill's bedroom door and rolled his wheelchair into the room to tell the prime minister that he had found the right name, only to find found Churchill standing stark naked from his bath. It is said that Churchill boomed, "Come in, His Majesty's First Minister has nothing to hide from the President of the United States!" Roosevelt had come up with the term "United Nations."

FDR and Churchill were in daily communication throughout the war. They met 9 times, for a total of 120 days. They got on well, indeed they became fast friends. The public saw the friendship; but it did not see the disputes. The priorities of the Britain and America were not the same: The United States wanted to end the war in the shortest possible time; so did Britain, but not at the expense of her vast colonial empire. There were severe disputes between the two sides over what to

do and when to do it. The two leaders worked as best they could with the Communist Stalin. The Russian leader did not trust either the Americans or the British. Nevertheless, the Big Three, Roosevelt, Churchill and Stalin, bound by their common objective to defeat Hitler, managed to hang together until victory was achieved. As Churchill put it in a note to FDR, ". . . a serious difference between you and me would break my heart and would deeply injure both our countries at the height of this great struggle." The Allies had to work together or all was lost.

Roosevelt saw his role as commander-in-chief and leader of the Grand Alliance as threefold: First. to hold the Alliance together; second to oversee all military operations; and third to keep America united in its determination to win the war. Working with Churchill and Stalin, FDR made the great decisions, decisions that affected the life and future of hundreds of millions of people across the globe. He appointed able military commanders who had his trust, as he worked to have theirs. He approved their strategy decisions but he did not meddle in their operations. He upheld the morale of the nation and the commitment of its people with biweekly press conferences, radio addresses and inspection tours of war facilities.

After the Japanese bombed Pearl Harbor, the nation was swept by rumors. Where would the Japanese strike next? If they could pull off the impossible task of bombing Hawaii, what couldn't they do? Would they bomb the West Coast, invade Hawaii or California? Acting in panic, fearing spies and saboteurs, the administration rounded up Japanese-Americans and Japanese permanent residents and interned them in camps deep within the western states. This shameful and racist act, approved by FDR, violated the Constitutional rights of these people in a most grievous manner. They were loyal Americans and many of their young men were released from the camps to fight side by side with their fellow Americans in the European campaign.

On the home front, Americans joined in the war effort. School children went door to door collecting old aluminum pots and pans to be used in the production of warplanes. People saved their grease and lard, which were needed in the manufacture of munitions. Food was rationed—meat, butter, eggs, coffee. Many families lived on a diet of Spam and Kraft cheese dinner. Clothes and shoes were rationed, tires, fuel oil, and gasoline too. Mothers hung small banners in their living room window with a star for each son who had gone to war. A silver star meant a son wounded in action, a gold star meant a son had been killed in the line of duty. Almost every city block had a small shrine that listed the names of residents serving in the armed forces. American coastal cities were under blackout regulations. Every home was required to have opaque window shades that were drawn down all the way at night to foil enemy bombers. Volunteer air raid wardens would knock on your door, should your lights be visible from the street. Life speeded up: the jitterbug, the lindy hop, the Jersey bounce became popular dances. The popular songs were patriotic: "Praise the Lord and Pass the Ammunition," "Remember Pearl Harbor," "Coming Home on a Wing and a Prayer," and, of course, Kate Smith singing "God Bless America."

For the duration of the war, the federal government managed the economy. Materiel and products were allocated to the military and the consumer markets by the government. Prices, wages, hours, and working conditions were con-trolled by the government. Travel space was allotted based on a priority system. As a result of these controls, the nation's economy operated throughout the duration—at maximum production, total employment, and vast expenditures—all without significant inflation or disruption of the American standard of living.

Industry went into all-out production, operating three shifts a day, seven days a week. U. S. production levels were amazing. People scoffed when Roosevelt set a production goal of 50,000 airplanes a year. FDR replied, with that supreme confidence of his, "Oh the production people can do it if they try." By 1943, the United States was producing more than a 100,000 planes a year. Ford's huge Willow Run plant, which built B-24 Liberator bombers, turned out one an hour. Ford also built more than a million military vehicles, including 277,000 jeeps. It took under a month to build a Liberty Ship, a full-size ocean-going freighter. Some were built in five days. More than 3,000 Liberty Ships were built over three years. Shipyard worker productivity, per man, went up an astonishing 40 percent per year.

Millions of young men volunteered or were drafted into the Army, the Navy and the Army Air Corps. Women too, joined up: the WAACs (later the WACs) in the Army, the WAVES in the Navy, the SPARs in the Coast Guard, and the WASPS in the Air Corps. WASP pilots ferried planes about the country, relieving their male comrades for combat service overseas.

The labor surplus disappeared quickly. Soon women were needed to fill what had been men's jobs. The popular song, "Rosie, the Riveter," signaled a step forward in women's rights. Rural African Americans streamed to northern cities to take defense jobs, and work side by side with their white coworkers. Black American soldiers served in every theater of war, albeit, in segregated units. Although races were still segregated in the South, Roosevelt issued an executive order on June 25, 1941, that banned all discrimination by reason of "race, creed, color, or national origin" in government and government contracts. He set up the Fair Employment Practices Committee to oversee enforcement. This, too, was a step forward in the struggle for equal civil rights for all Americans.

Roosevelt was even more popular as commander-in-chief than he had been as president. His "Dr. New Deal" had now become "Dr. Win the War." He and Eleanor worked hard to build confidence both at home and in the armed forces. FDR continued his reassuring fireside chats, carefully explaining what was going on to the American people. The president now traveled in a blacked-out train and under cover of total security, with an entire railroad car full of communications equipment. He made long cross-country trips inspecting war production plants and military camps. In an open auto he would drive down the assembly lines, stopping from time to time to talk with workers. The Secret Service would find an elevated spot for the president's car, so that he could address the assembled employees. This way FDR could speak from a sitting position and yet be seen by his audience. If no such spot could be found, the Secret Service would build a ramp for the car, sometimes as much as two stories high. Roosevelt would tell the gathered defense workers that his presence was a "little secret" that they must keep to themselves. When he made his unannounced inspections of army bases, he reveled in the startled looks of GIs, drawn up for review, when they realized it was the president of the United States inspecting their ranks.

Sometimes the secrecy cover of these trips was broken by Roosevelt's dog, Fala. A passenger train with its blinds dawn, waiting on a siding, while a Secret Service man, in a suit and tie walked a little Scottie dog—this was a dead giveaway. It is no wonder that the Secret Service code name for Fala was "The Informer." Fala was the most famous dog in America.

MGM even made a movie about his life, with the president as a supporting cast member. In fact Fala became a campaign issue in the 1944 election. Republicans falsely claimed that FDR inadvertently had left his dog behind on an Aleutian Island during his Pacific trip and had sent a Navy destroyer, at great expense, to bring Fala home. Roosevelt famously hammed it up in his response to the charge. "Republican leaders have not been content with attacks upon me, my wife or on my sons. No, not content with that, they now attack my little dog, Fala. Well I don't resent attacks, and my family doesn't resent attacks, but Fala does resent them. You know that Fala is Scotch and being a Scottie, when he heard the destroyer story, with its supposed cost of two or three or twenty or eighty million dollars—his Scotch soul was furious. He hasn't been the same dog since."

Eleanor Roosevelt stepped up her wartime activities. She became codirector of civil defense operations. She visited the wounded, she worked for the Red Cross, she labored ceaselessly to see that women and African Americans received a fair break in defense plants and the armed services. In 1943, she visited war torn Britain for two weeks, meeting thousands of GIs on a one-to-one basis and building good relations with our Allies. In 1944, she made an arduous trip throughout the South Pacific war theater of operations. She visited more than a hundred hospitals, talking with each and everyone of the wounded men. She spoke to thousands of soldiers and was seen by more than 400,000. Gruff old Admiral of the Pacific Fleet, Chester "Bull" Halsey was against her visit to the war zone and said so. By the end of her visit, he had changed his tune, confessing that, "She alone had accomplished more good than any other person, or any group of civilians who had passed through my area." Throughout her 7,000-mile journey, she continued to type out her daily newspaper column on her portable typewriter. When she returned to Washington, she gave a nationwide broadcast telling American families about how their loved ones were doing on the battlefront.

* * *

In North Africa, General Montgomery stopped the advance of Rommel's Afrika Korps at the great desert battle of El Alamein on November 2, 1942. From that point on, the British pushed the Germans back, step by step toward Tunisia. On November 8, American forces invaded Vichy French North Africa at three points. In sporadic yet fierce fighting across Morocco and Algeria, American forces under a young, new general named Dwight Eisenhower, linked up with the British to push the Germans out of North Africa.

By May 1943, the Germans had fled to Sicily. From there, they were driven back by Allied forces in fierce fighting up the boot of Italy. The puppet French government collapsed and the Nazis now had to occupy all of France, pulling valuable German troops away from the front. Across the occupied nations of Europe, from Greece to Norway, the Germans had to struggle with rising resistance from Allied-supported guerrilla forces. In a courageous move, the French Navy, loyal to the Allied cause, scuttled its ships rather than turn them over to the Nazis. The Allies now controlled the Mediterranean and the vital supply lines to the Middle East and mainland Asia.

On the Russian front, the battle was stalemated. The Russians seemed to have unlimited manpower. No matter how many men the Nazis killed, there were always more. The Russians have a saying: Russia has two great generals, January and February. The Russians knew how to fight in winter; the Germans did not. In the bitter cold of winter, both in 1941–1942 and in 1942–1943, the Soviets were able to retake the territory the Germans had taken in the summers. Hitler was furious. He sacked his commanders and took field command of the Russian campaign himself. In his madness, he commanded that his troops must not retreat or surrender. They must stand or die At the fateful battle of Stalingrad they did just that.

The Germans besieged Stalingrad. For six and a half months, the Germans fought the Russians street by street, house by house, staircase by staircase. They totally destroyed the city, dropping millions of bombs in saturation raids. In the middle of the winter of 1943, the Germans were surprised by two entirely new Russian armies, over a million strong, joining their comrades in battle. In a fiercely fought pincer movement, the Russian forces were able to surround the Germans. The Russians won in March 1943, capturing 22 divisions, 160 of the best trained units in Hitler's army. After Stalingrad, the Germans began their long and bloody retreat out of Russia.

In the South Pacific, American luck and skill began to turn the table on the Japanese. Most of the capital ships sunk or damaged at Pearl Harbor were raised and restored to service in short order. Japanese strategy had been to achieve their Pacific objectives in 1942, before the U. S. Navy was able to rearm and strengthen its fleet. This strategy failed. At the Battle of the Coral Sea, the Navy blocked the Japanese conquest of New Guinea. At Midway Island on June 4, 1942, the American met and sank the four aircraft carrier task battle group that had bombed Pearl Harbor. From Midway on, America was on the offensive in the Pacific. Roosevelt committed most of the American fleet and more than a million men to the defeat of the Japanese.

❊ ❊ ❊

The war came to its climax in 1944. In the Pacific, the leapfrogging strategy was working. The Japanese had spread themselves thin, occupying the widespread island chains across that vast ocean. Rather than fight island by island, American forces attacked major bases deep within the enemy perimeter, turned them into American bases and used them to cut supply lines to the remoter enemy bases. The plan worked but the Japanese proved to be tenacious fighters, willing to fight to the last man. In the defense of the island of Tarawa, for instance, out of 4,600 Japanese, only 17 survived to be taken prisoner. Leap by leap—Guadalcanal, Tarawa, Kwajalein, Eniwetok, Saipan—U. S. forces moved closer to Japan as MacArthur and his troops fought up the coast of New Guinea and in the East Indies.

In a great naval battle, nicknamed by the US Navy "the Marianas Turkey Shoot," the Japanese took staggering losses. Its fleet could no longer mount an offensive threat. On October 20, American forces invaded the Philippines. General MacArthur waded ashore to the land he and his soldiers had

been forced to evacuate almost three years earlier. "I have returned," he said.

Rome fell to the Allies on June 5, 1944. On D-day, June 6, 1944, Allied forces crossed the English Channel to invade Nazi-occupied Europe. It was by far the largest invasion in history: 3 million men from more than 25 allied countries, 11,000 aircraft, 4,000 naval vessels. In a broadcast on the morning of D-day, FDR led the nation in prayer, a prayer he had written: "Oh Lord, give us Faith. Give us Faith in thee; Faith in our sons; Faith in each other; Faith in our united campaign. With Thy blessing, we shall prevail over the unholy forces of our enemy."

Fighting through France and the low lands was no turkey shoot. Hitler in his madness, ordered his troops to "stand or die," and in the honored tradition of the Prussian Wehrmacht, they did. As the battles raged in France, Russia, Italy, the Philippines, and across the Pacific, it was election year at home.

With the nation in an all-out war effort, FDR's political enemies spread the rumor that he would call off the elections. When asked about this, Roosevelt responded, "How?" He flatly rejected the rumors, saying, ". . . these people around town haven't read the Constitution . . . I have." Certainly, there would be elections.

Over 1944, Roosevelt had been losing his physical strength and endurance. In a misguided effort to reduce his workload, doctors canceled his daily exercise routine. Under cover of wartime security, he stopped wearing his painful, heavy braces, stopped standing for photos and public appearance. As a result, his muscles, which he had so carefully trained to peak performance, withered in strength. The adhesions in his paralyzed leg muscles tightened up, making standing even more painful. His blood pressure became increasingly labile—under stress and fatigue, it would shoot up to dangerous levels. He would vary in his behavior. At times, he would be buoyant, at the top of his form, and then, at others he would sink into himself, staring blankly, seeing nothing, his jaw hanging slack. He lost weight, developed dark rings under his eyes and an ashy complexion. Nevertheless his mind remained clear, his judgment sharp, and his leadership steady.

He was a tired juggler. He was working closely with the temperamental Churchill and the darkly suspicious Stalin; with the heavy demands of his generals and admirals; with the always contentious Congress and the endlessly critical press—while at the same time supporting the confidence and morale of American troops abroad and the citizens at home. He was shouldering a burden of immense dimensions. He had been president through 12 years of mounting crisis and it is no wonder his body began to wear out.

Would he run again? The answer was yes. He was determined to see the war through to its conclusion and to ensure the creation of a United Nations through which he hoped future major wars might be avoided. He was running, he told his son James, " to maintain a continuity of command in a time of crisis. I can't quit in the middle of a war."

The strength of American democracy was demonstrated in the wartime election of 1944. Conservatives and former isolationists hated Roosevelt. They waged a well-organized, well-financed campaign. Their candidate, Republican Thomas E. Dewey, was a tidy little man who, it was said, looked like the groom on a wedding cake. Dewey whistle-stopped across the country saying "the Communists are seizing control" of the FDR administration. By voting against Roosevelt, Dewey said, "we can forever remove the threat of monarchy in the United States." To all of which FDR responded, "Now, really—which is it? Communism or monarchy?"

Roosevelt barely campaigned. As commander-in-chief, in July, he visited the Pacific war zone and, in conference with General Douglas MacArthur and Admiral Chester Nimitz, approved the strategy for the final phase of the war against Japan. He visited troops, inspected bases in Hawaii and the Aleutian Islands. Back home, he signed the GI Bill of Rights into law. This revolutionary act later served to change America forever.

In September 1944, Roosevelt met with Churchill in Quebec where plans were approved for the final push against Germany. It was not until September 23, 1944, that Roosevelt began his reelection campaign with his famous Fala speech. This was followed on October 21 by a campaign tour of New York City. The president overruled the Secret Service, who were appalled at the idea that he should break all security rules by making such a public appearance in wartime. Roosevelt, to counter the rumors about his bad health, spent fours hour in a cold, driving rain, riding fifty miles in an open car through New York City's five boroughs, waving to more than two million people who waited in the rain to greet him. The impact of the tour was spectacular.

In the last week of the campaign, FDR put on his tortuous braces to stand up and deliver four major speeches: in New York, Chicago, Philadelphia and Boston. This was the extent of his campaign. On election day, he won reelection to a fourth term as president, 432 electoral votes to 99. As he went to bed election night, Roosevelt was heard to murmur about his opponent, "I still say he's a son of a bitch!"

Franklin D. Rossevelt Presidential Library

For the first time in history, American women were accepted as members of the Army, Navy, Coast Guard and Marine Corps. Here FDR at Camp Oglethorpe, Georgia, April 17, 1942, reviews more than 3,000 women marching in parade, members of the Women Auxiliary Army Corps, commonly known as WAACs. Beside his car stands the corps commander, Colonel Oveta Culp Hobby.

Franklin D. Rossevelt Presidential Library

The Army was still segregated. At Camp Joseph T. Robinson, President Roosevelt arrives April 18, 1942. African American honor guards lining his route stand at attention as he drives by. Roosevelt attended Palm Sunday church service in the camp gymnasium with 3,400 of the black officers and men.

Franklin D. Rossevelt Presidential Library

Franklin D. Roosevelt Presidential Library

On the Chinese front, fighting was fierce, but the battle was at a stalemate. Mme. Chiang, wife of the Chinese leader, Generalissimo Chiang Kai-Shek, came to America to lobby for more military aid. Known to some as "The Dragon Lady," Mme. Chiang overstayed her welcome at the White House. Here FDR greets Mme. Chiang at Washington Union Station, February 17, 1943.

Franklin D. Roosevelt Presidential Library

During the War, Prime Minister Churchill and President Roosevelt met togeth-er a total of nine times, planning the grand strategy that stretched across the Atlantic, Europe, Africa, Asia, and the Pacific. Churchill and Roosevelt confer, January 18, 1943, in Casablanca, Morocco. Churchill holds his cigar while FDR's Camel cigarettes lie on the table.

Still Pictures Branch, National Archives and Records

American forces, under the leadership of Dwight Eisenhower, a new and untested general, landed in west Africa, November 1942. By May 1943, the Americans advancing from the west and British forces advancing east from Egypt, drove the Germans out of Africa. This victory, together with the Russian victory at Stalingrad, pushed Hitler back into his "Fortress Europe." This photo shows the American crew of an M-3 tank of the 1st Armored Division, under the command of Lt. General George S. Patton, Jr., at Souk-el-Arba, Tunisia.

Still Pictures Branch, National Archives and Records

On July 10, 1943, 500,000 Allied troops, carried by 3,000 ships, invaded Sicily. Thus began a long and bloody battle up the spine of Italy, that lasted the rest of the war. Here GIs dig up a buddy, buried under a collapsing building that suffered a direct hit from a Nazi bomb.

*Commander-in-Chief Roosevelt, General Eisenhower, Commander of Mediter-
ranean Forces, and, behind them, the famous tank commander, General George
S. Patton, in a photo taken December 12, 1943, at Castelvetrano in newly liberated Sicily.*

Franklin D. Rosevelt Presidential Library

*America poured men, planes and ships into the South Pacific. A leapfrog
strategy forced the Japanese back, from island chain to island chain—the
Solomons, the Marshalls, the Carolines, the Marianas. The fighting was dirty
and hand to hand. Casualties on both sides were enormous. This photo shows
U. S. casualties lying on stretchers aboard a lighter taking them to an offshore
hospital ship, July 12, 1943, New Georgia Island, in the southwest Pacific.*

Still Pictures Branch, National Archives and Records

On D-day, June 6, 1944, the Allies launched the largest invasion in history across the English Channel onto the beaches of France. Eleven thousand airplanes, many thousands of ships and boats, and close to three million men participated. This is a D-day view of Normandy Beach taken from a landing craft.

Franklin D. Roosevelt Presidential Library

Franklin D. Rossevelt Presidential Library

In July 1944, at the very climax of the war, FDR was nominated by the Democrats to serve a fourth term as president. He accepted in a radio address from San Diego, California, on his way to the Pacific theater of war. He was not a well man, as this photo shows, but he felt committed to serve for the duration of the war, along with the millions of Americans in uniform.

Franklin D. Rossevelt Presidential Library

In Hawaii, Roosevelt consulted with his Pacific commander. In this photo, he receives a briefing, flanked by General Douglas MacArthur and Admiral William F. Halsey.

On his return voyage, President Roosevelt stopped off at Adak, an island at the far end of the Aleutian chain of Alaska. American fighting men had recovered the island from Japanese occupation. Here FDR is shown having lunch with the enlisted men at the U. S. Navy mess hall.

Franklin D. Rossevelt Presidential Library

Eleanor Roosevelt travelled tens of thousands of miles visiting Army and Navy bases in Britain, South America and throughout the South Pacific. She made an enormous contribution to the morale of America's fighting men and women overseas. Here she stands in an Army chow line to get her dinner at a base on the Galapagos Islands in the Pacific Ocean.

Franklin D. Rossevelt Presidential Library

Franklin D. Roosevelt Presidential Library

Insert: NNMC, Bethesda

In spite of the war, the Polio Foundation, founded by FDR, continued to hold its Roosevelt Birthday Balls across the country to raise money in its fight to eradicate polio. This 1943 photo of such an affair shows Mrs. Roosevelt cutting the birthday cake surrounded by movie stars: Gene Kelly (on the far left); Veronica Lake and Joe E. Brown (eating cake); and Jane Wyman, then wife of Ronald Reagan; Myrna Loy; George Murphy (to the right of Mrs. Roosevelt); and child star Margaret O'Brien (in front).

The Naval Medical Center in Bethesda, Maryland, was built according to a design concept sketched out on a cocktail napkin by Roosevelt. These photos show the napkin and the building. FDR is shown leaving the Center in his 1939 Packard, after dedication ceremonies, August 31, 1942.

Franklin D. Roosevelt Presidential Library

Franklin D. Roosevelt Presidential Library

Commander in Chief Roosevelt spent only a few days on the campaign trail. To the horror of the Secret Service, he announced that he would drive through all but one of New York City's five boroughs in an open car on October 21, 1944. The day was cold and windy with a driving rain. Nevertheless, an estimated three million New Yorkers turned out to cheer their president. He did not disappoint them. Here he is shown riding rain-soaked in his open car

Franklin D. Roosevelt Presidential Library

Chapter *12*

Roosevelt and the Big Three

The president was not a well man. He seemed to know that he was dying. He asked Eleanor to gather all the grandchildren at the White House for Christmas 1944. As commander-in-chief, he ordered his eldest son, now Marine Colonel James Roosevelt serving in the South Pacific, to return for the inauguration ceremony, to serve one last time as his father's "arm." The ceremony was a short one, held on the back porch of the White House. There were no parades. "Who is there here to parade?" asked FDR. America's armed forces were fighting overseas.

Standing on his braces, he took the oath of office and gave a short three-minute inaugural address. During the speech he suffered an attack of angina—dreadful, burning chest pains radiating from the heart. Roosevelt did not flinch, and he finished the speech. After the ceremony, he took off his braces and never put them on again. He had stood for the last time. Before James returned to the Pacific, FDR gave him the family signet ring that he had worn since his father had given it to him many years before. James did not expect to see his father alive again.

FDR continued to direct the war in all its phases. He spent much of his time in bed—reading documents, thumbing

At the end of 1944, Roosevelt gathered all his grandchildren at the White House for Christmas. His four sons were absent; they were all overseas fighting for their country in the war

through newspapers, dictating to his secretaries and meeting with his advisors. He spent most weekends at Hyde Park, sitting by the fire with Daisy Suckley, his lifelong friend and confidante. She made the tea, and FDR toasted and buttered the bread. In spite of his growing fatigue, he maintained a busy schedule with press conferences, meetings with congressmen and foreign dignitaries. He might be weak and tired, but he remained firmly in charge.

In the spring of 1945, it was clear the war in Europe was drawing to a close. In the Pacific, American forces were massing for what would be the final phase of the war, a great invasion of Japan itself. Roosevelt's military planners were expecting as many as a million casualties in the battle. The time had come for the great powers to meet and coordinate, if possible, postwar plans for occupation of the enemy states and restoration of the governments of the liberated nations. Plans must be made for the accommodation of millions of refugees and the feeding of an entire continent.

In March 1945, the Big Three—Stalin, Churchill and Roosevelt—met at Yalta in the Soviet Crimea. Roosevelt traveled 7,000 miles to the meeting, first on board the Navy cruiser USS *Quincy,* and then by air from Malta to Yalta. This was the first flight ever made by an incumbent president. He flew on the C-54 plane named the "Sacred Cow." It had been converted for his use. The "Cow" had a conference room with a picture window, a bedroom and bath, and a specially designed wheelchair, small enough to navigate inside the plane. It even had a telescoping elevator to lift the president in his chair into the plane.

Each leader came to the meeting with a different agenda.

Stalin would allow nothing to interfere with Russian dominance over its neighbors, Poland and the Balkans. Churchill wanted full restoration of the nations of the British empire and British control of the Mediterranean Sea and Suez Canal. Unbeknownst to Roosevelt, Churchill and Stalin had cut a deal, dividing up southeast Europe, with Britain having control over Yugoslavia and Greece, while Russia would control Bulgaria and Roumania. Roosevelt had three objectives: free elections in Poland, Russian entry into the war against Japan, and Russian participation in the United Nations after the war was over.

Stalin did agree to open a mainland offensive against Japanese troops in Manchuria, thereby weakening Japan's defenses against an American invasion. He did agree that the Soviet Union would become a full-fledged member of the United Nations. He weaseled on Polish elections. It is doubtful that Roosevelt had many illusions that Communist Russia would allow its neighbor Poland to become a democracy with free elections and freedom of speech. In this regard, Roosevelt and Churchill held a weak hand. Russian forces were already in occupation of the country. The Russians had 12 million armed men in Europe, while the United States, Britain and the rest of the Allies had but 4 million. To remove the Russians from Poland would have taken a new war—a war for which Britain was too exhausted and America had no stomach. It was Roosevelt's hope, illusory perhaps, that Russia's aggressive policies against the democracies might be softened over time in a continuing dialogue at the United Nations.

Summarizing Yalta to an advisor, FDR said, "I didn't say it was good, I said it was the best I could do." Barely a week after his return, Roosevelt said, after reading the reports of Stalin's treachery in Poland, "We can't do business with Stalin. He has broken every one of the promises he made at Yalta." Such behavior, he cabled Churchill, was "unacceptable and if continued would cause our people to regard the Yalta agreement as having failed."

In his last public appearance, President Roosevelt reported to the Congress and the nation on the conference. FDR was exhausted. He looked haggard, his suit fit loosely on his frame and at times he slurred his speech. For the first time, he addressed the Congress seated in a chair, saying, "I hope you will pardon me for the unusual posture of sitting down during the presentation of what I wish to say, but I know you will realize that it is a lot easier for me in not having to carry about ten pounds of steel around the bottom of my legs and because of the fact I have just completed a fourteen thousand mile trip."

Eleanor was fully aware of Roosevelt's poor health and exhaustion. At the time, she wrote to an old friend, "I think he faced the fact, five years ago, that if he had to go on in office to finish his work, it must shorten his life, and he made that choice. If he can accomplish what he set out to do, and then dies, it will have been worth it. I agree with him."

In April 1945, Roosevelt went to Warm Springs for a week or two, to rest up and recover his energy after the long journey. Always before, Warm Springs had worked its magic and he had regained his bounce and vigor. It did not work this time. On April 12, 1945, at his beloved cottage, The Little White House, President Roosevelt suffered a cerebral hemorrhage and died. Working on a

speech, his last written words, penciled in the margin, were, "The only limit to our realization of tomorrow will be our doubts of today. Let us move forward with strong and active faith."

Every American who was alive the day Franklin Roosevelt died remembers where he was and how he felt hearing the news. For most Americans, the president had become a member of the family, a trusted, wise father figure. Grief was immediate and nationwide. Throughout the war, the *Washington Daily News* carried a box on its front page, listing the names of local soldiers and sailors killed or wounded in battle. On April 13, 1945, the name Franklin Delano Roosevelt was added to the list in the war casualty box.

Franklin D. Roosevelt Presidential Library

There was no parade at Roosevelt's fourth inaugural, January 20, 1941. "Who is there to march?" he asked. America's armed forces were overseas fighting a world war. FDR took the oath of office on the south portico of the White House. The president brought his eldest son, Marine Colonel James Roosevelt, back from the South Pacific to serve as his "arm" at the ceremony as he had done at the previous three inaugurals.

Franklin D. Rossevelt Presidential Library

Franklin D. Rossevelt Presidential Library

Three days after the inaugural, the President journeyed half way around the world to confer with Churchill and Stalin at Yalta, in Georgia, a Republic of the Soviet Union. They discussed the approaching end of the war in Europe and its aftermath, and the strategy to end the Asian-Pacific war. The Yalta decisions and disagreements shaped the world for over a half a century.

Franklin D. Rossevelt Presidential Library

On his return trip from Yalta, FDR conferred separately with three kings: King Ibn Saud of Saudi Arabia (left) and King Farouk of Egypt (right) and Emperor Haile Selassie of Ethiopia (not shown).

Franklin D. Rossevelt Presidential Library

Franklin D. Rossevelt Presidential Library

U. S. Marines are shown raising the flag over Mt. Surabachi after the brutal Battle of Iwo Jima in the South Pacific. This photo is signed by members of Easy Company, 2nd Battalion, 28th Marine Regiment, 5th Marine Division. Moments after this photo was taken, the scene was reenacted for press photographers. That photo became the model for the famous sculpture, the U. S. Marine Corps Memorial, in Washington, D.C.

Franklin D. Rossevelt Presidential Library

By March 1945, Allied troops had the Nazis on the run. German-occupied countries had been liberated, and the fighting had crossed into the German homeland. America began repatriating its wounded soldiers. In this photo, GIs, bandaged and disabled, greet the Statue of Liberty as their ship steams into New York harbor.

Franklin D. Rossevelt Presidential Library

Upon his return from the Yalta conference, the President reported to the Congress and the American people on the results of the meeting. For the first time in the 12 years of his presidency, the exhausted Roosevelt appeared in his wheelchair before the public.

Franklin D. Rossevelt Presidential Library

Shortly after his speech to the Congress, FDR went to Warm Springs, Georgia in a last attempt to regain his strength and energy. He died of a cerebral hemorrhage April 12, 1945. This last photo of Franklin Delano Roosevelt was taken the day before his death..

Today's Army-Navy Casualty List

Washington, Apr. 13—
Following are the lastest casualties in the military services, including next-of-kin.
ARMY-NAVY DEAD
ROOSEVELT, Franklin D., Commander-in-Chief. wife: Mrs. Anna Eleanor Roosevelt, the White House.
Navy Dead
Decker, Carlos Anthony, Fireman 1c. Sister, Mrs. Elizabeth Decker Metz, 16 Concord Pl., Concord, S.I.

Hundreds of thousands, if not millions, lined the railroad tracks, as the train bearing Roosevelt's body passed on its way from Warm Springs to his final resting place in Hyde Park. Here in Washington, D.C., the coffin is being transferred onto a horse-drawn U. S. Cavalry caisson for a solemn funeral procession to the White House, where the remains will lie in state for 24 hours.

Still Pictures Branch, National Archives and Records

Still Pictures Branch, National Archives and Records

Chapter *13*

Roosevelt, the Legacy

World War II ended as Japan surrendered on August 14, 1945. Across the country Americans celebrated "VJ" day. Nowhere was the celebration larger than in Times Square. Here, in this famous photo by US Army Signal Corps Lieutenant Victor Jorgensen, an unknown sailor sweeps an unknown nurse off her feet.

In his State of the Union message to the Congress in January 1944, Roosevelt laid out his vision of America after the war. In carefully crafted words, emphasizing key points, he called for "a second bill of rights" to assure to all Americans "equality in the pursuit of happiness":

The right to a useful and remunerative job in the industries or shops or farms or mines of the Nation;

The right of farmers to earn enough to provide adequate food and clothing and recreation;

The right of every businessman, large and small, to trade in an atmosphere of freedom from unfair competition and domination by monopolies at home or abroad;

The right of every family to a decent home;

The right to adequate medical care and the opportunity to achieve and enjoy good health;

The right to adequate protection from the economic fears of old age and sickness and accident and unemployment;

And finally, the right to a good education.

All of these rights spell security. And after this war is won we must be prepared to move forward, in the implementation of these rights, to new goals of human happiness and well-being.

FDR did not live long enough to lead the nation toward this vision. But he left us a road map.

In the decades since the deaths of Franklin and Eleanor Roosevelt, America has moved forward down this road.

In 1946, President Harry Truman appointed Eleanor Roosevelt as the first American delegate to the United Nations General Assembly. It was her dogged leadership that produced the United Nations Declaration of Human Rights, a document as important to the organization and to the developing nations around the world as the Declaration of Independence and the Bill of Rights are to America. It is now part of international law.

As envisioned by FDR, the UN has become the world's forum. The United Nations has taken on many functions. It serves as a broker between the great powers; it provides peacekeepers and peacemakers in regional disputes; it coordinates and distributes relief supplies to refugees and peoples at hazard. It serves as a clearinghouse for national codes on women's rights, minority rights, disability care, health, education, and welfare standards. Through the United Nations and its associated agencies, the ideals of Franklin and Eleanor Roosevelt continue to inspire action across the world.

Here at home, much that is good about America today is based upon the work of the Roosevelts. Americans are happier, healthier, and more secure because of their efforts. All America has access to electricity and telephones. Americans now reap the rewards of land reclamation and conservation programs, interstate highways, flood and disaster relief. Americans benefit from a social safety net: Social Security, Medicare and Medicaid, food programs, unemployment compensation, workers' compensation, regulated stock and bond markets, home mortgage assistance, insured bank deposits, the list goes on and on. Americans of all colors and creeds now receive the equal protection of their Constitutional rights, not just in theory but in fact. All of these things had their roots in FDR's New Deal.

A great national memorial has now been built in Washington, D. C. The Franklin Delano Roosevelt Memorial takes its place beside the Washington, Jefferson, and Lincoln Memorials. The FDR Memorial is like the man, simple and close to nature. It is like a walled garden of four open rooms, symbolizing Roosevelt's four terms in office. The memorial has trees, shrubs, and flowers; water pools and waterfalls; and glorious views of official Washington. At its entrance is a statue of Roosevelt, the man, life size, seated in his wheelchair, wearing his old campaign hat and his pinch glasses. Behind him rise the walls of the memorial commemorating the achievements of this man in a wheelchair throughout his four terms. Upon these walls are carved quotations from his writings and speeches.

Over the decades since the New Deal, Americans have lost the spirit of togetherness that the Roosevelts inspired. Under their leadership, citizens joined in common cause to improve the living standards of all. It was this national unity that enabled the United States to organize and fight World War II so effectively. Perhaps, over the last decade or so, the nation has begun to regain some of this lost spirit, some of this Roosevelt confidence that problems can be confronted, confronted and solved if we work together. On the last wall of the FDR Memorial are carved the president's last written words, "We must move forward with a strong and active faith."

The great luxury ocean liners were converted into troop ships during the war. Here HMS Queen Mary *enters new York Harbor carrying thousands of GIs returning home in 1945 after victory in Europe. The* Mary, *now in dry dock at Long Beach, California, is a popular tourist attraction.*

Still Pictures Branch, National Archives and Records

Christened by his widow, the aircraft carrier USS Franklin D. Roosevelt *was commissioned October 27, 1945. The ship saw active duty during the Korean and cold war years.*

Franklin D. Rossevelt Presidential Library

THE TEST... WE ADD MORE TO THE ABUND... WHO HAVE MUCH; IT IS WHETHER ... ENOUGH FOR THOSE WHO H... FRANKLIN D. ROOSEVE...

Franklin D. Roosevelt Presidential Library

Franklin D. Roosevelt Presidential Library

No longer first lady, Eleanor Roosevelt continued as an active national leader in the civil rights movement until her death in 1962. Here with famed actor/activist Harry Belafonte, she dedicates a plaque in 1959. It reads, "The test of our progress is not whether we add more to the abundance of those who have much; it is whether we add enough to those who have too little." These words were spoken by Franklin D. Roosevelt in his second inaugural address, January 20, 1937.

In 1946, President Harry Truman appointed Eleanor Roosevelt as the first American delegate to the United Nations General Assembly. Here she confers with fellow delegates Adlai Stevenson and John Foster Dulles. Stevenson was Democratic candidate for president in 1952 and 1956. Dulles served as President Eisenhower's Secretary of State, 1953–2959.

This mural, by artist Conrad A. Albrizio, illustrates how FDR is remembered in the United States. FDR and his New Deal brought new security, dignity and prosperity to the working men and women of America. This mural, The New Deal, was commissioned for the Leonardo da Vinci Art School in New York City. It was painted under the auspices of the New Deal Federal Arts Project. Such works of art are now a national treasure of great value.

Franklin D. Rossevelt Presidential Library

Franklin Delano Roosevelt with six other presidents

Franklin D. Rossevelt Presidential Library

Assistant Secretary of the Navy Roosevelt with his boss, mentor, and hero, President Woodrow Wilson. Also in the photo is William Jennings Bryan, four time Democratic candidate for president. Bryan is in white, Wilson wears a dark jacket, and FDR has on a three-piece suit. Wilson was president, 1913–1921.

Franklin D. Rossevelt Presidential Library

Young State Senator FDR at a 1901 reception greeting ex-president Theodore Roosevelt on his return from his expedition to Africa in search of big game. FDR is the straw hat to the far right. His Uncle Teddy is in the foreground left. Theodore Roosevelt was president, 1901–1908. (photo edited)

Arch political foes, President-elect Franklin D. Roosevelt and outgoing President Herbert Hoover, March 4, 1933. The ride to the Capitol for DFR's inauguratioin was a chilly one—scarcely a word was said. Hoover was president, 1929–1933.

Franklin D. Rossevelt Presidential Library

A 1944 campaign shot of FDR with his vice presidential candidate, Harry S. Truman. No one was more surprised than Truman when FDR chose him as VP. Roosevelt was in poor health, and Truman did most of the campaigning in that year. Truman was president, 1945–1953.

Four star general Dwight David Eisenhower with his Commander in Chief, Franklin Roosevelt. Eisenhower had won his stars in the African Campaign. FDR chose him to command the Allied invasion of Europe, June 6, 1944. Eisenhower was president, 1953–1961.

Lyndon Baines Johnson was an ardent young New Dealer from Texas. FDR took an interest in the new Congressman and campaigned on his behalf in Austin, Texas. Johnson was president, 1963–1968.

The Franklin Delano Roosevelt Memorial was dedicated May 2, 1997. This is an aerial view of the memorial taken by its designer, the acclaimed architect Lawrence Halprin. A statue of FDR seated in his wheelchair is now in place at the memorial's entrance.

Suggested Reading

Burns, James MacGregor Burns, *The Lion and the Fox*. New York: Harcourt, Brace & Co., 1957.

Cook, Blanche Wiesen, *Eleanor Roosevelt: Volume I, 1884–1933*. New York, Viking, 1992.
       Eleanor Roosevelt: Volume II, 1933–1938. New York: Viking, 1999.

Freidel, Frank, *Roosevelt: A Rendezvous with Destiny*. Boston: Little, Brown & Co. 1990.

Gallagher, Hugh Gregory, *FDR's Splendid Deception*. Arlington VA: Vandamere Press, 1999.

Goodwin, Doris Kearns, *No Ordinary Time: Franklin and Eleanor Roosevelt: The Home Front in World War II*. New York: Simon & Schuster, 1994.

Kennedy, David M., *Freedom from Fear: The American People in Depression and War, 1929–1945*. Oxford: Oxford University Press, 1999.

Suggested Reading (continued)

Leuchtenburg, William E., *Franklin D. Roosevelt and the New Deal*. New York: Harper & Row, 1963.

Morgan, Ted, *FDR: A Biography*. New York: Simon & Schuster, 1985.

Roosevelt, Eleanor, *This I Remember: The Autobiography of Eleanor Roosevelt*. New York: Da Capa Press, 2000.

Ward, Geoffrey C., *Before the Trumpet: Young Franklin Roosevelt, 1882–1905*. New York: Harper & Row,1985.

Ward, Geoffrey C., *A First Class Temperament: The Emergence of Franklin Roosevelt*. New York: Harper & Row, 1984.

Index